Richard Aldington: An Intimate Portrait

Richard Aldington

An Intimate Portrait

EDITED BY

Alister Kershaw

AND

Frédéric-Jacques Temple

Southern Illinois University Press

Carbondale and Edwardsville

Preface

A GLANCE at the bibliography appended to this volume gives some idea of the astonishing range and diversity of Richard Aldington's work and, in an age when illiteracy is regarded as a positively desirable quality in writers, perhaps accounts to some extent for the neglect from which his books have suffered during recent years. Novels like *Death of a Hero* and *Very Heaven* show Aldington to have been an "angry young man" long before today's self-pitying intellectuals bestowed the term on themselves, and his anger, greater than theirs and rooted in a deeper experience, was expressed with a passion which they have never equalled. At the same time, he was capable of a sort of bitter compassion as in *The Colonel's Daughter* or *Women Must Work,* while in *All Men Are Enemies* he achieved a unique lyrical sensuousness. C. P. Snow has rightly emphasized the impossibility of "pinning him down" as a novelist, poet, essayist, or translator, and, similarly, it is impossible, within any of these various genres, to catalogue him as belonging to this or that school, as consistently adopting this or that approach. This is particularly evident in his scholarly works: *Literary Studies and Reviews* and *French Studies and Reviews* (It is worth noting, incidentally, that so distinguished an expert as

v

Professor Gustave Cohen has paid tribute to Aldington's unrivalled knowledge and understanding of French literature.) show him to have been as responsive to Proust as to the anonymous poets of the thirteenth century, as quick to appreciate Remy de Gourmont as Landor.

In his translations, too, just as he was equally at home in French or Italian, Greek or Latin (not to mention Provençal or medieval Liégeois), he displayed the same vivid perception and skill whether he was dealing with texts by Anyte of Tegea or Boccaccio, Euripides, or Voltaire. Scholarly precision is likewise reflected in his biographies. He has been accused—quite falsely—of having deliberately set out to "debunk" but he was as incapable of setting to work with any such *parti pris* as he was of writing servile "official" biographies. His only concern was to examine the available material with the utmost objectivity and to follow where the facts led. His reputation as a "debunker" is founded solely on *Lawrence of Arabia* and the somewhat waspish recollections of Norman Douglas recorded in *Pinorman;* his critics prefer to overlook the respect and admiration which he showed in his biographies of D. H. Lawrence, Voltaire, and the Duke of Wellington. It was not Aldington's fault that an impartial investigation of Lawrence of Arabia proved the "national hero" to have been largely a fraud; one might even have thought that it was to his credit that he was prepared to set down the facts while knowing that he would have to face just such hysterical abuse as was eventually levelled at him. The whole key to Aldington's work, indeed, lies in his unfashionable passion for truth: in his novels, poems,

vi

and biographies, it was always the "image of integrity" which was paramount.

RICHARD ALDINGTON was born in Kent, England, in 1892 and educated at Dover College and London University. Before the First World War, he was the youngest of a group of writers which included Ezra Pound, Wyndham Lewis, H. D. (who became his first wife), F. S. Flint, T. S. Eliot, and D. H. Lawrence, and is generally regarded as a leader of the so-called "Imagist Movement." Aldington always denied that this "movement" ever consisted of more than a few poets who had independently reached more or less similar conclusions about the way in which they wanted to write. Nonetheless, it is a fact that those involved, whether linked in a movement or not, had a significant influence on the subsequent direction of English and American poetry.

The "Bohemian" life of London, brilliantly described in the early part of *Death of a Hero,* was terminated in 1914 by World War I. Aldington enlisted as a private in the British Army and was later commissioned in the Royal Sussex Regiment. After being demobilized in 1919 he worked for some years as a critic of French literature on the *Times Literary Supplement* and contributed to various other reviews while still continuing to publish such volumes of poetry as *Exile, A Fool i' the Forest,* and *The Eaten Heart.* His international reputation, however, dates from 1929 with the publication of *Death of a Hero,* widely regarded as the greatest of war novels.

Like his friend D. H. Lawrence he was ill at ease in

postwar England, and his success as a novelist enabled him to leave the country more or less permanently. Thereafter he lived mostly in France and Italy, although rarely staying very long in any one place and travelling from time to time in North Africa, the West Indies and America. The outbreak of World War II found him in the United States where he remained until 1946 when, after a short stay in Jamaica, he returned to Europe. In 1947 he settled in the South of France, first at Le Lavandou and then in Montpellier. Ten years later he moved to a tiny hamlet outside Sury-en-Vaux in the Cher where he died on 27 July 1962.

His last five years were spent in almost complete isolation. Aldington no longer wanted to see any but a handful of close friends and, as far as the Anglo-Saxon "literary world" was concerned he was virtually a forgotten man. The only tribute to this most individualistic and least "committed" of writers during his latter years came from Russia where, a few weeks before his death, he spent a month as the guest of the Soviet Writers' Union. It is because they believe that one of the outstanding literary figures of our time has been unjustifiably neglected in the English-speaking world that the editors offer the present volume to the public.

Acknowledgments

THE EDITORS wish to acknowledge the permissions granted to reprint the following published works. The review written by Roy Campbell appeared as "The Happy Pagan," *The Poetry Review*, XL (April–May, 1949), and is reprinted by permission of Mrs. Mary Campbell. The article written by Harry T. Moore was published as "Richard Aldington in His Last Years," *The Texas Quarterly*, VI (Autumn, 1963), and is reprinted by permission of *The Texas Quarterly*. The poems quoted by Sir Herbert Read are reprinted by permission of Madame Catherine Guillaume née Aldington. The contribution by C. P. Snow is taken from the pamphlet "Richard Aldington: An Appreciation" by C. P. Snow, and is reprinted by permission of Lord Snow and William Heinemann, Ltd.

The article written by Henry Williamson appeared in *The Aylesford Review*, V, No. 4 (1963). The article by Dilyara Zhantieva was published in the magazine *Soviet Literature*, No. 12 (December, 1962).

Contents

Notes on the Contributors

SAMUEL BECKETT, author and playwright, was born in Dublin in 1906. He was educated at Portora Royal School and Trinity College in Dublin. He has lived mostly in France since 1947. He has written many poems, short stories, novels, and plays. Among them are the well-known plays *Waiting for Godot* and *Krapp's Last Tape.*

ROY CAMPBELL, born in Durban, South Africa, was a poet and critic. He served on the Literary Advisory Board of the B.B.C. from 1945 to 1949. He made extensive lecture tours and was the author of many poems and prose works, including an autobiography, *Light on a Dark Horse,* 1951. Roy Campbell died in 1957. The review reprinted in this volume appeared in the *Poetry Review* in April–May, 1949.

RICHARD CHURCH is a poet, novelist, and literary critic. He began writing at eighteen and published his first book of poems, *Flood of Life,* in 1917 when he was twenty-four. He has written numerous novels and poems and contributed reviews to the *Spectator. Over the Bridge,* the first volume of his autobiography, was awarded the *Sunday*

Times Prize for Literature in 1955. The second volume, *The Golden Sovereign,* was published in 1957.

PAVEL CHUVIKOV, born in 1906, is the author of a number of books, pamphlets, and articles. For almost fourteen years he was the head of the Foreign Literature Publishing House and, in that capacity, was among those Soviet men of letters who welcomed Richard Aldington to the Soviet Union. He is now Director of the All-Union Book Chamber.

LAWRENCE DURRELL, poet and novelist, was born in India in 1912 of Irish parents. He is a former member of the British Diplomatic and Information Services. He has written novels, volumes of verse and humor, and numerous magazine and newspaper articles. He achieved worldwide fame with his *Alexandria Quartet.* He edited *The Best of Henry Miller* in 1960.

T. S. ELIOT was an essayist, playwright, and educator. Richard Aldington was his assistant editor when Eliot started the *Criterion* in 1921. Eliot was awarded the Nobel Prize for Literature in 1948. He was a Clark Lecturer at Trinity College and a Charles Eliot Norton Professor of Poetry at Harvard. He received the Hanseatic Goethe Prize in 1954. His most successful plays were *Murder in the Cathedral* and *The Cocktail Party.* T. S. Eliot died in January 1965 in London.

JOHN GAWSWORTH is a poet, bibliographer, and the coordinator of the Neo-Georgian lyric poetry movement in

1937. He was the editor of the *Literary Digest*, 1946–49; editor of the *Poetry Review*, 1948–52; and acting editor of *Enquiry*, 1949. Among his many publications are *The Dowson Legend, The Invisible Voices,* and *Snow and Sand*. He is the editor of some sixty verse collections and volumes of prose.

SIR WILLIAM HALEY has been editor of the *Times* since 1952. Before that he was for nine years Director General of the British Broadcasting Corporation. As a young man he wrote literary articles under the name of Joseph Sell and, as a result, came to know Richard Aldington.

ALISTER KERSHAW was born in Melbourne, Australia, in 1921. He is the author of various volumes of poetry and prose. He settled in France in 1947 and for some years was Richard Aldington's private secretary. He is now Paris correspondent for the Australian Broadcasting Commission. Aldington spent the last five years of his life in Kershaw's house in central France.

THOMAS MAC GREEVY was born in 1893 and educated at the University of Dublin. He is an Officer of the Legion of Honour, Cavaliere Ufficiale al Merito della Repubblica Italiano, D. Litt. (Honoris Causa), National University of Ireland. Until 1963 he was director of the National Gallery of Ireland. He is the author of some verse and numerous critical articles and monographs, including *Richard Aldington: An Englishman*.

MORIKIMI MEGATA was born in Kyoto in 1921. He was educated at Kyoto Imperial University and Kyoto University. He is Assistant Professor of English at Kobe City University of Foreign Studies. At present he is engaged in research in Oxford and Cambridge. He has contributed to a number of learned Japanese publications.

HENRY MILLER, novelist, was born in New York City in 1891. While living in Paris from 1930 to 1939 he was European editor of *The Phoenix*. He is the author of many books including the controversial *Tropic of Cancer* and *Tropic of Capricorn*. His book, *Black Spring,* was published in the United States in 1963.

HARRY T. MOORE is a Professor of English at Southern Illinois University. His best known works include *The Life and Works of D. H. Lawrence* and *The Intelligent Heart: The Story of D. H. Lawrence*. He is the author of a book on John Steinbeck and a reviewer of literature for the *New York Times* and *Saturday Review*. He is the general editor of a series of literary critiques published by the Southern Illinois University Press.

LAWRENCE CLARK POWELL, librarian and author, is dean of the School of Library Service at the University of California (Los Angeles). He has traveled widely as a lecturer and written many books, including *Books in My Baggage*. He contributes articles and reviews to various literary, historical, bibliographical, and library periodicals. He was director of the Williams Andrews Clark Memorial Library when Aldington lived and worked in Southern California.

SIR ALEC RANDALL was in the British Diplomatic Service from 1920 to 1952. He was assistant to Ford Madox Ford in writing his two war books. He served as secretary of the British Legation to the Holy See, Rome, 1926–30; First Secretary of the British Legation to Bucharest, 1933–35; British Ambassador to Denmark; and delegate to the United Nations, 1952–58. In 1956 he published a volume of reminiscences entitled *Vatican Assignment,* and in 1960 a guide to Rome called *Discovering Rome.* He was a college classmate of Aldington and remained a friend until Aldington's death.

SIR HERBERT READ is director of George Routledge and Sons, publishers, a post he has held since 1939. He was a Watson Gordon Professor of Fine Arts at the University of Edinburgh, lecturer in art, University of Liverpool, Charles Eliot Norton Professor of Poetry at Harvard, and A. W. Mellon lecturer in Fine Arts, Washington. He was created a knight in 1953. Among his many books on art and poetry are *To Hell with Culture* and *The Contrary Experience,* both published in 1963.

C. P. SNOW, novelist and physicist, was chief of scientific personnel for the Ministry of Labour during World War II. He has written many books on a wide range of subjects, including a cycle of successful novels portraying English life from 1920 onward. His book *The New Men* won the James Tait Black Memorial Prize in 1954. He became Lord Snow in 1964 and is now Parliamentary Secretary to the Ministry of Technology in the British Government.

FRÉDÉRIC-JACQUES TEMPLE, French poet and writer, was born in Montpellier, where Richard Aldington spent many years. He is the author of many works including *D. H. Lawrence: l'oeuvre et la vie* and *Inferno*. He has translated various works from English and edited a collection of tributes to Roy Campbell entitled *Hommage à Roy Campbell*. He is a contributor to numerous French and foreign reviews. At present he is Director of Programs, Radiodiffusion-Télévision Française, Montpellier.

MIKHAIL URNOV, born in 1909, is a literary critic, scholar, and translator, specializing in British and American literature. He is a Professor of Literature at the Moscow Institute of Printing Arts and a member of the Soviet Writers' Union. He collaborated in writing the *History of English Literature* for the Soviet Academy of Science and was co-author (with D. M. Urnov) of *Shakespeare: His Heroes and Time*.

ALEC WAUGH was born in London in 1898. He spent many years travelling or in the military service, from which he retired in 1945 with the rank of major. He is the author of over forty books which include *Island in the Sun,* 1956 (also produced as a film); *In Praise of Wine,* 1959; and *Fuel for the Flame,* 1960. He has travelled extensively as a lecturer, and was the editor of works of Charles Dickens including *The Pickwick Papers* in 1959.

HENRY WILLIAMSON, author and journalist, was born in 1895. He has been constantly writing since 1921. His first publication was a tetralogy called *The Flax of Dream* formed by *The Beautiful Years,* 1921; *Dandelion Days,* 1922; *The Dream of Fair Women,* 1924; and *The Path-*
xviii

way, 1928. Over the years he has written numerous books and articles, the latest of which is *The Power of the Dead* in 1963. The article in this volume appeared in *The Aylesford Review* in 1963.

DILYARA ZHANTIEVA, born in 1906, is a specialist in modern English literature at the Gorky Institute of World Literature of the Soviet Academy of Science. She is a contributor to the *History of English Literature* and the author of a number of books and articles. She wrote the preface to the English-language edition of *Death of a Hero,* Aldington's book which was published in the U.S.S.R. in 1958.

Illustrations

Richard Aldington: An Intimate Portrait

Samuel Beckett

J'ai moins de souvenirs que si j'avais six mois. Among the ghostly few is that of the great kindness shown to me, in Paris, in the late twenties and early thirties, by Richard Aldington. My first two publications, by Hours Press and Chatto & Windus, I owe in part to his good offices. I think of him with affection and gratitude.

Roy Campbell

That a similar state prevails in the arts to-day to that which prevails in the overstaffed bureaucracies is proved by the vast preponderance in bulk of an irrelevant and parasitical literature of theory, explanation, and criticism which entirely overshadows and dwarfs the creative work around which it was originally written. In various branches of the Civil Service, employment has to be artificially faked for a huge mass of pen-pushers who are entirely superfluous to the original function of the department which employs them. This spurious secondary employment, because it nourishes a vast majority of pen-happy clerks becomes the main activity of the department: and the necessary purpose for which the department was originally founded becomes a subsidiary sideline existing only by permission and under the authority of the superfluous majority. A new language of officialese has to be invented (comparable to the meaningless technical jargon of contemporary criticism) to give the illusion of reality and necessity to this world of fake-

4

employment which nourishes them. In literature the poet (that is the minority-man who is still performing the function of literature) depends for his contemporary fame and perhaps his livelihood, largely on whether his work can be used to illustrate the pet theories of the uncreative majority of politico-critical pedants who really for the time being call the tune. As Richard Aldington points out in his brief and masterly introduction to his collected poems, commentators on verse are more interested in discussing what they call "tendencies" than on studying the work of the poet. One crossword-conscious pedant has the effrontery to tell us that he likes his poetry "difficult," as "something to be wrestled with," and for every clear-headed poet, like Aldington, there are at least three hundred crossword-conscious professors demanding, like this one does, to be *puzzled* by poetry which is more difficult to read than to write; poetry in which they can joyfully hunt the thimble of meaning through haystacks of self-bamboozlement; poetry which is vague and formless but offers (like Leonardo's mildewed wall) a million suggestions of half-meanings and glimmerings of sense. Whenever the reader, the listener, or the spectator wants, as in this case, to join in the show and "be clever too" he crashes a great donkey's hoof through the whole function of art and reduces it to collective barbarism and imbecility. Aldington does not cater for this collective craving. There is not enough hesitancy or obscurity in Aldington's work to nourish a single one of these parasitic interpreters, or employ even a part-time hack-translator of verse into literary officialese, the function of the modern critic. He is his own commentator; his verse, even though concerned with great pro-

5

funditties of thought and feeling, is always explicit and clear. It is for his earlier rôle as a daring innovator that he has received more recognition than for his subsequent achievements as a poet, which entirely eclipses his earlier, better-known, anthologised work. It is only on reading this magnificent collection of work written during the last thirty-five years, that one realises how shamefully one of the best of living poets has been neglected: and also that in Aldington's case (as in the rare cases of Hardy and Lawrence) a first-rate novelist has been equalled if not excelled by his own achievement as a poet.

In his introduction he tells us that, in his experience, poetry was not the result of selfconscious effort but seemed to occur quite spontaneously and mysteriously. "That is the moment of poetic ecstasy," he tells us, "which almost invariably occurs in a mood of what Wordsworth called 'wise passivity'—all the rest is hard work." At a very early age Aldington was already endowed with such lapidary skill as a chiseller of poetical medallions, that he was able to discard the traditional aids to poetic form from the outset. By dint of sheer "hard work" that skill has become a second nature: so that under the stress of passions which tend to make most other poets long-winded by discursive love, anger, or hate it enables him to find the fullest expression in the fewest possible words. Brevity, with him, is not only the soul of wit, but of passion. Though he has written long poems of perfect construction, like *The Dream in the Luxembourg, A Fool i' the Forest* and *The Crystal World,* they are formed, like crystals, of smaller crystals, each of which is a separate whole, brief and crisp as an epigram.

6

Aldington was one of the first English poets of this century to discard the conventions of rhyme and metre, which were unnecessary to him. The vast majority of English poets have since discarded these conventions for looser and freer forms which are easier to write, but which often prove that the discarded conventions were of as great a necessity to them as a bellyband to a fat man. Aldington discarded them for a stricter and more difficult form which can hardly be called free verse because of the masterful control which regulates and balances every detail with the minutest precision: and which enables him to perpetuate moments of illumination in forms as hard and clear as gems, which, nevertheless, retain the warmth, fragrance, and freshness of the first impulse to write. If we compare his verse with much other rhymeless and metreless verse, we begin to see what rhyme and metre were originally intended for. The rhymes were intended as hurdles, ditches, and hedges, to tire out long-winded poets so that they would soon lose their breath and shut up. The metre was apparently intended to serve to the average poets' thoughts as a corral serves to a herd of jungle-happy nanny-goats to keep them from rambling, and straying, and getting lost. Together rhyme and metre acted as a sort of corset to Muses who suffered from Elephantiasis of the Soul (as they usually do when they have little to say).

Though Aldington was one of the few who originated the whole movement of what we call modern verse, he took no part in any of the commercially collectivised *"movements"* or *"tendencies"* during the nomadic inter-war period when almost every article was headed "towards a new synthesis," "towards" a new this, "towards" a

7

new that, and "towards" a new the other; every review and every magazine, with the same stale and mouldy monotony that christens Tea-shops "olde," was christened New:—*"New* Roads," *"New* Trails," *"New* Tracks," *"New* By-passes," *"New* Highways," *"New* By-ways," etc., until this Ye Olde Newnesse became a pain in the neck: and one yearned for some review to be called "old" by way of novelty. A *New* newness was needed. There is no doubt it was intended, by the number of different sorts of roads that were mentioned as "New," to suggest some kind of vast unrest, a nomadic or migratory "movement." But there wasn't the slightest "movement" *"towards"* anything: the illusion of "movement" or "tendency" was kept up by violently marking time in perfect goose-step. Step was changed simultaneously in perfect time—always toeing the line of financial expedience. Nothing else could explain the sudden simultaneous conversion (as soon as it was expedient) of peace-time belligerents into war-time cushion-bashers: and of fire-eating bolsheviks into mealy-mouthed apostles of a theosophoid and buddhistified travesty of anglicanism which bears about as much relation to Christianity as the Boy-scout Movement does to the Regular Army. How all these neck-spraining volte-faces can happen so suddenly and simultaneously without causing a single broken neck or even a loss of balance anywhere, is quite easily explained by the fact that by sheer hard practice double-facedness has become as much a second nature to this *"school"* of poets who ruled the roost for twenty years, as skill became to Aldington through hard work. And it was a *"school"* in more senses than one:—

8

"O Sunrise, bare-kneed captain of my first school,"!!!
lisped one of these grizzled and superannuated Billy Bun-
ters who was acclaimed for this or similar flights, by that
indefatigably oily trickler of unction, Mr. Cyril Connolly,
as the "MONT BLANC" of CONTEMPORARY ENGLISH POETRY,
towering over the heads of his contemporaries. If we look
up any of the poetry periodicals of that epoch we will find
(as in a copy of *"New* Verse" which I have here before
me) that the poets of that time who were most in the
limelight were preoccupied almost entirely with what was
either politically or morally *unreal* i.e., Utopias or Vices:
and they had developed a critical jargon to deal with these
subjects which is comparable to the abracadabra of superfluous government pen-pushers in dealing with the printed
forms whose only purpose it to give them employment.
Aldington had no contribution to make to this false paradise. In a fake-world where Mont Billy Bunter represented
the "ceiling" as it were, and soared in snow-clad majesty
over the rest of the surroundings, there was no room for
anything like Aldington's verse. He did not mix business
with inspiration: he did not do anything that got one into
the limelight of the book trade: he never banqueted for
"democracy" in the rearguard in Spain: nor preached a
bogus egalitarianism in which its own most fervent poetical exponents believed less than anyone else, and of which
they only practised the very opposite; he had in fact be-
haved at one time like a *black-leg* and *practised* a sort of
human equality (instead of merely preaching it) by serv-
ing his country in the ranks, sharing their lot with his
fellow men, and skulking away there in the trenches—
when he should have been boldly holding the fort with his

9

eating-irons as a chairborne parasite-trooper in the Knife-and-Fork Brigade, like the Billy Bunter set-up did in this last war. It is no wonder that he was ignored: but a wonder he was not boycotted for the straightforwardness and honesty of his work, since he has many a laugh at the literary claptrap of an age in our past literature. He could not interest anybody in a *tendency* "towards" anything for he had long ago found his way to where he *is;* and (thank God!) he is not likely to try to develop a *"tendency"* in order to attract the unburied corpses of an abortive generation such as ours has done its best to become. They say no man can fully savour and enjoy living until he has thoroughly experienced love as a lover, poverty as a poor man, and war as a soldier. That is to say the more one has enjoyed, experienced, and suffered the more zest it arouses. I should add religion to the other three volcanic fountains of power and joy, and put it first: but I notice that Aldington seems to have the same feeling about religion and religious people as I have about pagans and free-thinkers, namely, that they are a puritanical crowd of kill-joys, teetotallers, cowards, dyspeptics, eunuchs, communists, suicides, vegetarians, pessimists or hypochondriacs; and for every unhappy Christian writer he could show me I could give him half a dozen cases of delayed birthcontrol, delayed demise, or, to descend from the sublime to the ridiculous (hold your noses, boys!)—delayed burial like the unutterable panegyrist of Mont Bunter! However that may be, it is a delightful experience, which makes me revise some of my views, to meet in Aldington the one example I know of a happy pagan writer who enjoys life although (no, rather *because*) he has seen and

10

felt a rougher side to it than our modern moaners, as one can see from his war poetry: who wears his vast erudition and scholarship lightly and gracefully, without pedantry; whose mature experience is not sour or vinegary but has the tartness of the real ripe apple of knowledge from the garden of Eden. He has written some of the finest love poetry of our time. He has none of the collective disillusionment which for so many years sold both itself and the public so successfully. One reads him not only for the poetry but for the companionship and comradeship of the man whom we feel to be so brave, sincere, generous, and full of charm. Robert Frost is the only other poet who gives me the feeling that I know him personally, as Aldington does, though I've never met either of them. His poetry has been obscured for us by the fake-screen of "movements" and "tendencies" for the last generation. But now it has come to us all together, and for good!

> *And if one day is trampled underfoot*
> *Or another forced awry or another stunted,*
> *Still there are days and days and golden days*
> *Like aconite-stars under the grey heaven of olives.*

Richard Church

The longer one knows a friend, the more difficult is it to describe him or her. Every human being is nine parts a mystery, one part a social organism discernible and comprehensible. There are some people, twisted perhaps by strange rigours and environments in childhood, whose personalities are even more elusive. Richard Aldington was one of them.

I first met him in 1921, at a moment when he was about to disrupt his life and to change the whole course of his destiny. The scene was a small Italian restaurant in Frith Street, Soho. A small party was gathered in an upper room to discuss the setting up of a new magazine, to be called the *Criterion*. The focal person, the chairman of this meeting, was Mr. T. S. Eliot. The others were Herbert Read and myself, both young Civil Servants already eagerly practising the art of poetry and educating ourselves toward that process; F. S. Flint, the Imagist poet who worked with me in the Ministry of Labour; Alec Randall and J. B. Trend who represented respectively the German and the Spanish interests in this new venture. All these members had in prospect distinguished careers in the arts, in diplomacy or university life.

While the supper was being discussed along with the literary problems, the door opened and a tall, upright figure appeared and walked silently over to the table, towering above it and looking down with a proud, aloof glance at each of us. He was Richard Aldington, at that time known principally as a promising young critic of considerable scholarship, especially in the history of eighteenth and nineteenth-century French literature. It was generally believed that he was ear-marked by the Establishment (if there be such a body) for the later Editorship of the *Times Literary Supplement* when Bruce Richmond should relinquish that important post. Now here he stood, obviously tense, keyed up, almost defiant. "I am on my way to Paris," he said, after he had been introduced to those of the group who had not met him before. I was one of them. I studied him as he spoke, and was conscious of an even deeper defiance than was patent in his appearance. His voice trembled as he added, "I am leaving England."

I think none of us missed the full intention underlying his words, and we were startled, embarrassed. This was a personal exposure, indicating a crisis. We felt, at least I did, that we were being blamed for something connected with this decision. It was as though he were contemptuous of all this: the literary activity, the eagerness and hopes of this group of English writers setting out on a new venture with this magazine which was to lift the standard of literary criticism, and to offer a platform for creative work not likely to find an outlet in existing journals. The history of that magazine is well known.

As far as I recollect, Richard Aldington did not join us. He stood and talked with us, at large, for awhile, and then walked out again, leaving us uncomfortable, enquiring of each other what this meant. We were soon to know. He had disposed of his library, left the woman with whom he had shared a cottage in Berkshire since the end of the First World War, deserted the *Times Literary Supplement,* and was off to Paris to settle there and to start a completely different kind of professional life as a writer. The first fruits of that was his famous novel *Death of a Hero,* which put him on the road to prosperity and fame both in Europe and America.

He never lived in England again, and returned here only for brief visits. Few of us saw much of him here. He lived in Paris and in the south of France, and was much in contact with D. H. Lawrence toward the end of Lawrence's life. He went to Hollywood, and lived for a time in Jamaica. I had long letters from him, much more affectionate and generous than he ever allowed himself to be in personal contact. Always there was about him an air of irritation, as though the momentary events and affairs of daily life were too much for his nervous system. He had a permanent frown. But behind it, especially during a tête-à-tête, with no third party present to complicate the relationship, there lay a character of wide interest and a slightly melancholy generosity; an odd mixture that both attracted and withstood the normal approaches of friendship. I must confess that I found him a lovable man, though he could be infuriating, especially when he unleashed his Anglophobia, a disease that smote him, possibly, out of the draughty corridors of the Department of Inland Revenue. And there were other reasons of a more domestic nature.

In 1946 I went to Paris for the first time since the end of the war to meet Aldington on his return to Europe. Our mutual friend, the dramatist Halcott Glover, was already installed there in a studio in the Rue Campagne Première, and there Aldington arrived with his young daughter, a pretty child of eight years. His wife was following by plane the next day. Aldington looked nervous, apprehensive. Europe for him was strange after so long a parting. He was guarded in his talk, as though confronting strangers who might accuse him of I know not what. To ease the tension, the Glovers and my wife and I took Aldington and his child to see Gordon Craig, who was living in a studio in Passy. Craig had a daughter there, a girl of about ten years of age, who already displayed the wonderful Terry vocal genius. In French and in English her words dropped from her lips like jewels from a casket. I listened enraptured, while trying to attend to the general conversation and to show enthusiasm for Craig's incunabula and puppets. The children went off together, and Aldington at once rose to a more carefree stance. It was obvious that he worshipped his daughter, and in consequence, at that stage in her growth, she drove him nearly mad.

Aldington was soon installed in a studio in Boulevard du Montparnasse, and while we were in Paris that month we saw much of him and his wife there. Much of his time was spent in worrying over the non-arrival of his books, which had been crated from Hollywood. Ultimately they came, somewhat damaged by damp, and he rented a handsome villa at Le Lavandou on the Riviera. I had one long spell of several weeks there in the autumn of 1947, after two severe operations, and this close contact with him during my convalescence revealed more of his character than I had apprehended during the many previous years since I first met him. His conversation, as we sat over long luncheons and dinners, drinking the local wine and cracking walnuts after the meals, was rich in experience and scholarship. But he was still Anglophobic and anti-political. This bitterness of soul contrasted oddly with his personal kindness and understanding. Our friendship ripened into a sincere affection and I returned to England with a sense of loss and dismay. However, we corresponded, even after he had removed to Montpellier following the breakup of his marriage. The world began to pass him by, largely because he ceased to do any creative writing, and he took to producing critical studies of people he had known, some of them now immortal, such as the two Lawrences, the criticism taking on an element of malice that reacted on his reputation. So he died more or less an exile, certainly from his own country, and from many of his friends. But for me he remains as I learned to know him at Le Lavandou; a noble figure, reserved but intimate, generous and tender, still displaying a passionate devotion to the art of letters.

Pavel Chuvikov

Address to Richard Aldington on the occasion of celebrations for his seventieth birthday in Moscow, 8 July 1962, from the Publishing House of Foreign Literature.

Dear and much respected Richard Aldington,

The Publishing House of Foreign Literature warmly congratulate you, a remarkable writer and a very dear friend, on the glorious anniversary of your 70th birthday. We are happy to have the opportunity of congratulating you here in the Soviet Union where millions of readers know you and love you. The breadth and youthfulness of your writings, their true humanity and anti-militarist feelings, bring your books to the hearts of a very wide circle of readers, to the hearts of the whole of progressive mankind.

Your novels, *Death of a Hero, The Colonel's Daughter, All Men are Enemies,* are very popular indeed among Soviet readers. We, the staff of this Publishing House, are

17

proud that last year we published a very large edition of your collected stories under the title *Farewell to Memories* —short stories which had not before appeared in Russian. These stories, written like your other works, vividly, with great skill, and great courage, have had an enormous and well deserved success.

We greatly appreciate your feelings of friendship and sincere goodwill towards our country, where readers love you and your books. We believe that our friendship and understanding will grow and strengthen.

Wishing you, our dear friend and guest, wealth, strength, long and fruitful years of life, and success to all your endeavours.

Pavel Chuvikov
Director of the Publishing House

Lawrence Durrell

Aldington's work meant a great deal to me as a young man and I was heartily glad to have the opportunity of trying to repay my debt to him by friendship and literary support during the last few years of his life when his fortunes had failed him and his career had virtually come to an end. I owed him much. Long before I could limp in French, his fine translations gave me a passport to French literature; his own war poetry and vivid satirical novels delighted me; it was in his pages that I first read serious praise of Eliot, Proust, and Joyce as the true creative spirits of our time. He had not waited until Lady Chatterley set the world by the ears to acclaim Lawrence; but had long since defended *The Rainbow* and *Sons and Lovers* in brilliant fashion. Pound and Lewis and Campbell also benefited by his strong sword-arm at a time when the general public looked upon them as noisy freaks or intellectual perverts, or worse.

All this was of the greatest importance to a writer in

the bud. His lively and compassionate views on literature were expressed in admirably fashioned prose, full of a fierce generosity which gave the lie to humbug and sterile pedantry. He occupied, from quite an early age, a well-merited position of importance in English writing and a thoroughly well-earned financial success with work on several fronts at once. All this is forgotten today but will soon be remembered when his books once more come into print.

At the time when I met him, disaster had overtaken him and financial distress stared him in the face—a serious matter for a man in his sixties, born and bred to literature, and who knew no other trade. He could not cheerfully turn to grave digging or teaching as I could—he had never been forced to do anything but write. His books on T. E. Lawrence and Norman Douglas were responsible for this state of affairs; they had not only damaged him critically but had alienated him from the common reader, from his own public, from the libraries. With the trouble caused by these two volumes the whole of the rest of his admirable life work went out of print and out of public demand—some seventy titles in all! This was, of course, catastrophic for a man living on his books, and he was facing up to it gamely; but the tide had turned against him. Publishers would not reprint him, booksellers would not stock him; but worst of all his public had deserted him. If his last few years were made tolerable and even happy ones it was due to the timely help of a fellow writer who also admired him and who set him on his feet financially.

He was a difficult, touchy, strange, lonely, shy, aggravating and utterly delightful man. I was very much honoured to enjoy his friendship and an intimacy which permitted me frequently to disagree with him. Curiously enough he enjoyed this very much. It never affected our firm friendship; and in fact he positively revelled in the title we (my wife and I) bestowed upon him—that of "Top Grumpy." He sometimes put on special performances of outrageous grumpiness specially for us, for the pleasure of making us laugh. And we tried more than once to coax him into some public field where his truly endearing grumpiness could cause sympathy and not distaste. Aldington would certainly have won both sympathy and attention had he attacked such a public medium. One could not help seeing the heart of gold underneath the surface explosions of temper; the generosity hidden under the snappy tone of voice. None of this, alas, can be done for one by cold print in default of the author's tone of voice, the connotation, the attitude of mind expressed by feature. Aldington with his striking good looks and gentle address would have been a winner. But he was too shy, and considered it "infra dig to make a mountebank of himself"—so I could only murmur "Touché" and leave it at that.

I have said he was lonely, and this is true; while he knew and loved Europe, spoke excellent French and Italian, one always thought of him rather as a British exile than as a European of British *souche*. He had cut himself off in some indefinable way from the current of British life, and in my view this isolation was harmful to this most British of authors. But here I stumble upon a field of absolute ignorance, for he was also a reticent man. He never spoke about his private life, his marriages, his personal affairs; indeed to this day I do not know anything about him as a human being, only as a writer. He once or twice hinted that his whole interior affective life had come to a stop in the twenties, and that after that epoch "everything seemed finished." Europe, he said, had committed suicide in 1914. I reminded myself that his first visit to Europe had been around 1905—an epoch which I have great difficulty in visualising.

Another factor which came into play due to his isolation was a curious though intermittent faulting of judgment in literary matters; of course he was deeply embittered by the collapse of his career. But he persisted in attributing it entirely to the fact that he had been ambushed by the critics and not cold-shouldered by the public. Nothing I could say would convince him that in the case of his Lawrence and Douglas books it was more his manner than his matter which had caused so much offence, which had indeed damaged the public image of this fine poet and man of letters. No. He would not have it. It was "The Cockney Commorra." The late Wyndham Lewis also suffered from this "secret enemy" complex—perhaps we all do to various degrees?

His death came as a great blow to us; there was nothing to predict it in his magnificent physique and his robust good health. I am inclined to attribute it simply to the fact that he felt there was nothing more to live for; he despaired of regaining the lost ground. For the last few years he had been living up in the Cher as the guest of a firm friend, admirer, and fine writer, who had put his house at Aldington's disposal. But most of the time he was alone, doing his own cooking. But he was proud as well as reticent and in all the long letters we got from him there is plenty of grumpiness but never a complaint. He went down with all guns firing, and his last letter which I received twenty-four hours before he died is full of rogue elephant fireworks; a specially grumpy performance deliberately calculated to make my wife exclaim: "Ah, that wrong-headed old grumpy up there in the Cher." I can hear his burst of laughter at the familiar phrase!

It was ironic that shortly before his death he was invited to spend his seventieth birthday in Russia and meet his Soviet readers. He went with a number of prepared grumpinesses and some specially tailored clothes designed to show that while he loved Russian literature and the Russian people he was Richard Aldington, Esq., British and Conservative to the core. But the warmth of his reception quite won his heart; readers from all over Russia slogged up to Moscow to shake his hand. I think in his heart of hearts he must have compared this reception to the grim silence of London—not one telegram of congratulations, not one line from the press!

Well, he is dead, this old British grumpy; subtract what you will on the account of wrong-headedness, of intemperateness of judgement, and so on. There remains a good deal which those who knew him will always remember with affection: great generosities, great quixotries, great gallantries. And when the smoke of battle has died down around his name, his books will win him back his true place among the important writers of our time.

T. S. Eliot

I met Richard first in 1917, just at the time when he was being drafted into the Army and I took over the assistant editorship of the *Egoist* from him. After the war I saw quite a lot of him. We were on very friendly terms and when I started the *Criterion* in 1921 he became my assistant editor at a very modest salary. (I, myself, took no salary at all because I was on the staff of Lloyds Bank and it was forbidden to members of the Bank staff to have other regular paid employment.) I think that in those years we exchanged quite a long correspondence and I visited him at least once when he was living with a lady, whose name I have forgotten, at Aldermaston—a village which was still very rural and had not acquired its recent associations. Richard was very sensitive, not to say touchy, in some ways and I am afraid that with good intentions, but clumsy lack of imagination, I hurt his feelings once or twice very deeply indeed. After that, I saw nothing of him and he wrote a cruel and unkind lampoon of me and of my wife who died some years later, and of friends of mine such as Lady Ottoline Morrell and Virginia Woolf. But then he was living, I think, in France and his attacks on other authors, the two Lawrences and Norman Douglas, were more direct in books about those writers. But that quarrel had since subsided and I exchanged letters with him a few years before his death. He had heard that a number of my letters to him were in the possession of a certain American university and wrote to me to explain that this was by no wish of his own, but that the letters had been in a box which he had left in charge of a man who he supposed to be a friend and who later denied having any such box in his possession. I have no reason to doubt his word and have nothing left but feelings of friendliness and regard.

I hope this brief communication is better than nothing. We were on the same side for a long time and I was the first to give offence, although unintentionally, which made a breach between us.

John Gawsworth

It seems impossible to realise—when reading a friendly news-crammed letter penned, within hours of his sudden death, from Sury-en-Vaux, on 26 July last, and ending "ever yours Richard,"—that I never met Richard Aldington in the flesh!

It is true that for nearly a quarter of a century—at intervals—we had corresponded: I generally in the rôle of suppliant editor, he in that of kindly mentor to one twenty years his junior, but of similar unorthodox, unfashionable tastes and fierce, proud prejudices. There was always talk of a meeting—but alas, it was not to be. Nonetheless, aside from our correspondence, friends common to us both fanned our friendship by word-of-mouth message as a score of years flashed by. From this panoramic pageant I hear their voices ring out: Roy Campbell's, Lawrence Durrell's, Nancy Cunard's, Henry Williamson's, Alister Kershaw's. Indeed it is not without difficulty that I can refrain from mesmerising myself into the belief that I have talked, and still do talk, with R. A. himself. Fanciful? But no, I think not. For to Aldington, as will be seen, I owe inestimable personal debts, such as I can never repay. Others will write here of his achievement. Such high assessments are beyond my range. Inveterate old diabetic bookman, slipper-padding around my shelves and files, for my small part I will cull some typical paragraphs from his letters here, and leave the reader to imagine their recipient's initial joy when those missives thudded through his letter-box to lighten a leaden-skied day in a maniac metropolis. No ark rang with happy hosannahs on a dove's green delivery as my heart pealed *Laus Deos* at the sight of Richard's spidery holograph I can still swear, hand on heart.

What have we here in this folder? No letters of the winter of 1939–40, when I reprinted his "Young Authors Beware!" extracted and "digested" from *The Star,* in the January (the seventh) number of my newly-founded *The English Digest,* certainly. This is not surprising; fire bombs destroyed my office at 38 Furnival Street in the Holborn blitz.

It is Peace again: 22 December 1946. Richard is in Paris, at 162 Boulevard du Montparnasse, recently laurelled with the James Tait Black Prize for his *Wellington,* and I am back from the R.A.F. and editing my new experiment, *The Literary Digest.* I have dug into old numbers of *Everyman* of the early thirties and discovered two "lost" Aldington articles eminently worthy of resuscitation. R. A. is agreeable.

22/XII/1946 Of course I shall be very pleased for you to print a summary of the article on Greek love poetry. I had entirely forgotten its existence, and was somewhat startled by the melodramatic title "The Perished Poems of Greece," until it occurred to me that this may be a bellyache about the destruction of the Greek lyrists by those vile Byzantine Priests. It is a good idea to call attention to the evils of fanaticism.

26/III/1947 I too was very glad that [Oliver] Onions got the J. T. Black Prize. He has done excellent work, and the way he is ignored and sneered at by the "high-bruffs" is most repulsive. I did feel glad Edinburgh snubbed them while honouring him.

By all means use anything of mine that is of any use to you. And don't forget to look us up here when you are next in Paris.

24/V/1947 By all means use the article on Gosse. I had forgotten all about it.

I look forward to seeing you in Paris soon, where conditions are not so evil as a sensational press pretends.

An interval of eighteen months ensued. Aldington had removed to the Villa Aucassin, St. Clair, Le Lavandou, Var; I was about to score my hat trick, and edit three journals, *The Literary Digest, Enquiry,* and *The Poetry Review* simultaneously. For this last I request contributions.

6/XII/1948 I'm afraid I can't send you any poems: there were only a few unpublished and an edition of my *Complete Poems* now in the press has scooped those in too. But I'm enclosing two translations [*The Vigil of Venus* and *The Syrian Dancer*] which you might care to have: they have appeared in America but never in England.

It is good news that you've taken over the editorship of

The Poetry Review and I look forward to seeing your first number. A journal without any regard for the cliques would seem to me to be very definitely one of the many things England needs. By the way, I wonder if you have thought of including anything by Rachel Annand Taylor? She is a poet of such great merit and it's monstrous that her work is not readily available. It is one of my greatest regrets that I missed her in compiling my anthology. I do penance for that every second day.

With very best wishes for the success of the *Review*.

27/XII/1948   You have worked like a hero to get that first number together so quickly.

It seems to me there is a great opportunity for a really catholic periodical dealing with poetry, avoiding cliques and the provincial poetaster, but giving specimens of modern verse of all kinds with articles and notices of English, American and Continental poetry. There is an immense area to be covered and your one difficulty is to collect a team of competent writers, while using your own judgment in picking outsiders and new writers.

My own belief, which I have backed heavily, is that people are sick to death of this more or less phoney "new writing" which is largely a means for concealing the fact that the writers have nothing worth saying. I believe there is a public which would welcome something wider than this wearisome repetition of a few well-worn names and any honest attempt to widen the circle of contemporary poets while keeping them informed of reprints, new editions, etc.

11/II/1949   Many thanks for the copy of *The Poetry Review*. Well, you certainly worked heroically to get that out, and deserve a laurel crown, not to mention more substantial rewards.

I'm sorry about Favonus [in *The Vigil of Venus* translation]. Mixture of bloody ignorance and carelessness. If I thought Gilbert Murray really liked my version I'd be considerably puffed.

He is the only living translator of the classics worth a damn, though the asses won't have it.

The old Roy [Campbell] is a gorgeous fellow. He sent me a most comical letter he wrote those xxxxx on *The Times Lit. Supp.,* and he seems to have written you something pretty lively. Matador be damned—he's one of the four or five greatest toreros of Spain. And of Provence too. You and I are nothing much down here, but they worship Roy.

Thank you for sending the check to Heinies. But get it straight, brother. The ban comes from England, not from France. The freest etc. country won't allow a check to be cashed abroad except by kind permission of the Bureaucrats. Here the *mot d'ordre* is "Resist the bureaucrats" as in England it appears to be "Lick their boots."

16/IV/1949   You are doing very well indeed with *The Poetry Review,* and I have a feeling Harold (Monro) would greatly approve. It was an excellent idea to round up the ancients before proceeding with your task of producing moderns out of the hat. I am delighted to see [Wilfrid] Thorley still going— I consider his versions of French poetry the best ever made on such a scale and equal in poetic merit to Helen Waddell. (Are you going to include her?) And F. L. Lucas, whose Greek Anthology pieces are excellent.

How is it that Shane Leslie appears to my astonished eyes as bartified as the pompous xxxx? Was he born in the purple of commerce or has he risen from the ranks of the aristocracy? I have now lived so long in republics that all contemporary titles seem more than a little ridiculous—especially in a national-socialist state.

Roy [Campbell]'s piece [*Richard Aldington, Happy Pagan*] is an admirable *basso profundo* of masculine invective—so superior in its warm-hearted growls to the spiteful squeals of the pansies. He is too generous to me, but there is no harm in that, for others have been very much the reverse.

When next you revisit the civilised world you must come and eat a bouillabaisse with me—at the moment we can even serve it with a perpetual accompaniment of nightingales.

10/V/1949   I see only one mistake in this proof [of *The Syrian Dancer,* Copa Syrisca, attributed to Vergil], but I daresay after it appears some obvious blunder will manifest itself from the ambush in which it has been lurking. This isn't a good version— Helen Waddell's is much better.

Who is xxx? Povero io! I have never heard of him, nor have I read his review, though Kershaw mentioned it was in the last batch of cuttings, said it was a re-hash of *T. L. S.* and probably by the same ass. Why bother about these people? They do not influence the real reading public, only a few hundred highbrows who are such a bore they would die of inanition if they weren't dead already without knowing it.

I am slogging away here nearly as hard as you in London, finishing up a biography which I hope will greatly annoy the highbrows by its content and still more by the fact that it will be an international success and make me lots of money! My last novel, where I had some fun with Casanova, has just sold out an edition of 49,000 in Czechoslovakia, and a large impression will soon be out in Italy. So why on earth should I worry about *The New Statesman?* They should worry about me! (Hope they do—pass it on to the silly cows.)

Quite a scurry of visitors of late—Kershaw and riotous Australians, Bill Dibben the bibliophile, Henry and Christine Williamson, old Roy's daughter due today—tell him we'll do anything we can for her. Henry is already tanned old oak colour, wearing Provençal labourer's blue cotton togs, and trying to figure out how to live on a hundred francs a day. Says he can't write here, but the rest and change are good for him. He takes life and England and himself too seriously. Insouciance, my boy, that's the word. And write what YOU want to write and what amuses YOU, and nuts to the highbrows. He who can, does; he who cannot goes on the B.B.C.

Ciao!

P.S. I'd love to have your *Collected Poems* if you can spare a copy. I read much poetry, some every day, but I'm damned if I'll read this ambiguous crap now fashionable which is the result of having nothing to say and not knowing how to do even that.

18/vi/1949 Congratulations on the hat-trick, but I'm afraid I'll have to refuse your suggestion [of contributing to *Enquiry*]. I'm in the middle of re-writing a book—125,000 words of it—and after that have promised myself a rest—the first for two years. You'll understand the position.

I've not heard from your wife but if she's anything like me she won't be interested in moving a yard from where she happens to be in the Var. It's too hot to move anyway.

Kershaw asks me to give you his greetings: he's just arrived back after a brief stay in London, was sorry not to see you there.

Best wishes for all three of your journals. Why not take over *Horizon* and see if you can make something of it?

24/xi/1950 This is very kind of you, and I wish I could respond. Perhaps you noticed that the last edition of my poems was entitled *Complete Poems*—which was intended to convey that I shall publish no more verse. In fact I have not published any since 1938, and am far better content to be a reader than a would-be writer of poetry. It is always pleasant to belong to a minority.

The two little verse translations I sent you for your opening were hurriedly made one evening in 1945 in California for an Anthology of Verse in Translation I did for the *Encyclopaedia Britannica,* which was then (and perhaps still is) owned by the University of Chicago. They paid me 1250 for this work, and have not yet issued it, though they keep threatening!! I hope they won't do it. The American Libraries are very poor in poetry, particularly verse translations, and I had to use some hideous stuff; nor have I time or inclination to revise the thing.

If there is any topic on which I might do you a bit of prose, I should be most happy to try.

Did I ever tell you that by great good luck I managed to obtain a copy of your edition of [*Theodore*] *Wratislaw* with your signature? It lives with my cherished rarities.

The next year found Aldington at "Villa les Rosiers, ancien chemin de Castelnau, Montpellier, Hérault."

I had myself been rusticating, in Shepperton and Ewell, and from the latter I wrote inviting him to support a Civil List petition for the author of *The Smoking Leg*. He was immediately sympathetic.

28/VI/1951 I am shocked and grieved to learn that a writer of Mr. Metcalfe's great attainments should be in financial difficulties, and enclose the signed document as I don't know the address of the Civil List people. (Probably it is 10 Downing Street, but this is one result of living out of England for so long.) I do hope you will be immediately successful in your generous effort and that Mr. Metcalfe will be relieved of all anxiety.

In October, 1955, I returned to London, and practically amphibian in Paddington's Little Venice, I breasted out for the third time on the sea of matrimony. Aldington had heard of the venture; a cheque arrived from a country bookseller, who owed him money, to provide a Wedding Breakfast, together with a Paean of a letter from the donor, which was evilly filched from me before it was even re-read. But in kindness Richard was ever continuous. From a note, dated 26 January 1961, addressed to him at Sury-en-Vaux, Cher, I find I am again in his debt for support-ing a Civil List Pension petition I had put forward for the widow of Philip Lindsay. A copy of my *Collected Poems,* out of print since 1949, was on the way to him with a possible view to a selection being made if the text in any way attracted him. From Sury, he wrote:

11/III/1961   I seem very slow in answering your letter of 26 Jan. "25 Castle Street, Dover" is the address of my solicitor brother's office. . . . I leave here on Monday for the South of France en route to Venice where I expect to be for a few weeks, having a literary job which can only be done there. I asked my brother to send on your books, but they have not arrived.

I don't think I am the person to re-introduce your poems. If not England's Literary Public Enemy Number One, I'm pretty high on the list since I published the facts about their favourite (and most mendacious) pansy hero, T. E. Lawrence. T. S. Eliot or Robert Graves would do the trick for you.

Excuse brief and rather confused letter, written in between bouts of packing, and attending to last minute jobs and callers.

21/VI/1961   You will long ago have condemned me as the skunk of skunks for this interminable silence. A really ex-traordinary series of mischances. At first my solicitor brother (who kindly takes some of my mail) did not understand that I wanted the books forwarded. He received my letter on the very day that he fell ill, and his chief clerk neglected to post them. Only when Tony returned to his office did he discover they hadn't been sent. Meanwhile, I went down to the Camargue to see my daughter and then went to Venice. It was over five weeks more when they caught up with me, as I was packing to return to France. As I was flying from Venice to Nice I had to send my books by post to lighten my valise. I sent your books to myself

chez ma fille, meaning to read them at once, and lo! they were
held up by the French customs and arrived just after I had left.
They eventually caught up with me here, just as I was involved
in a "rush" job to write the new article on *Wellington* for an
American Encyclopaedia and also with a lot of dull letters about
"rights" for two paperbacks reprints in U.S.A.

Anyway, I'll go through your poems carefully, and will select
60—though you could do it better. I am amused by dear old
Roy's article, as he wrote a very similar one about me. Evidently
it was his formula when reviewing his friends—to attack their
imaginary enemies (really his own) and to say as little as possible
about the poems.

On the 24th I have let myself in for a week's motor drive
round France (with the peasants blocking the roads) with a
friend to whom I rashly made a promise months ago.

I'll let you have the selection as soon as I can. . . . Larry
Durrell would be a better sponsor for you than I can be. He lives
near Nîmes.

8/vii/1961   I am glad to be in direct touch again. The
above address will always find me, even when I am away since
I make arrangements for re-forwarding. For the next two months
or more I plan to stay here, for the roads are much too dangerous
with drunken trippers and Parisians who think themselves "superior" and hence break all the road rules simply because they live
in a large, noisy, smelly and insanitary town.

You must try to get the special number devoted to "Banabhard" (Rachel Annand) who was vastly superior to the herds
of time-servers who high-hatted or ignored her. *Leonardo* sold
vastly in U.S.A.—I used to see it constantly in the shops there—
but owing to some blunder in her contract she was never paid
for it. In some mysterious way Roy received a lot of her letters
in a legacy of someone's library. Unluckily, he lost or destroyed
many of them, but gave me all he had left, and I have them
stored in the attic here.

Venice is still Venice, though one has to do a lot of avoiding of Americans, Swiss, Belgians and Germans who permanently occupy the area round Piazza S. Marco. But with patience and a little knowledge they may be avoided. On my last day I wandered for three or four hours in quite unspoiled calli and campi between S. Stae and the Zattere, and I think did not meet one foreigner until I got right across.

I'll make the selection as soon as I can.

14/VII/1961   Herewith the selection from your poems, given by their numbers as you suggested. As a matter of fact the selection has to be arbitrary, as there is not a bad poem in the book, and a selector can only go on personal taste which may not be that of others. In handling the sonnet you rival Roy and Banabhard. I gave the Cleopatra pieces complete, both for their achievement, and because I think they should not be broken up.

Would you not like me to return the copy of your *Collected Poems,* from which I made this selection? I seem to remember you said it is your last copy, and it has stuck in that very characteristic piece by Roy. Just let me know and I'll return it, unless you can assure me as you have the whole thing in duplicate.

19/VII/1961   Have you not received my letter with selection of your Poems? If not, tell me, and I'll repeat. Shall I return book? Very sorry indeed to hear of your illness, and hope so much you are better. Desperately busy, and visitors just about to arrive.

31/VII/1961   I have had guests en série, a new lot arriving just as the former departed. Now I have my daughter and her young man, and must give up tomorrow to take them to Vézélay. I "profit" as they say here by a respite.

I am concerned by what you say of your health. Should you not have an operation for the hernia? I had to have one pre-1914, only too successful since I always passed A 1 fit for active service. Doesn't the Hellfare State have to look after you gratis? Or do you rank as a fascist beast?

I told you my selection was entirely personal. Use it if you wish, and if you dislike, scrap it. The person who could help you is Larry Durrell—a big name in the trade now . . .

4/IX/1961   Herewith the blurb duly authenticated with me own moniker. I particularly want that bit about "not one bad poem in the collection," because the more I read, the more the fact interested me.

Have you followed up my suggestion and asked our old friend Larry Durrell to give the selection a leg-up? I may be seeing him before long in the Midi, and if he doesn't do something I shall brand his forehead with the word "LOUSE"! Like Dante.

Coincidence. By the same post as your letter I received from an American publisher a cheque (correction—check) for advance on a new paperback edition there of my book on *D. H. Lawrence,* and a letter from my agent passing on a perfectly acceptable offer for an American paperback for my *Cyrano de Bergerac* which first appeared in 1922! So in spite of the kindly efforts of "critics" to sink them our little paper boats do sometimes re-appear on the surface! . . .

I didn't know there was a Rachel Annand Memorial. There ought to be a collective "Hommage" such as we did for Roy in France. The British proved what lice they are over that—only one or two Catholic and Fascist papers noticed it. Yet, even Dame Edith was a contributor. But to hell with the lit'ry British —they hate us youth. Ever yours Richard [A stain] O not beer, alas, but tea!

A complete breakdown in the spring of this present year, 1962, forced me to relinquish a two years' endured employment on urgent medical advice, and a kindly proposal was then mooted for a book of tributes to be collected for my benefit, moral and financial, a *Festschrift* designed to coincide with my fiftieth anniversary. The editor approached R. A. On his return from the U.S.S.R., where his own seventieth anniversary had been widely and warmly celebrated, this letter and one from me, suggesting that that unique sculptor, Oloff de Wet, who particularly delights to honour poets, immortalizer of Dylan, of Roy, of Blunden and, just at that instant, of myself, might immediately fly to France to do his bust and Durrell's, awaited Aldington's reply. The cheerful missive that follows casts no shadow before, gives no hint of his immediately impending death, which occurred so suddenly the next day . . . not a suggestion of fatigue informs it or, for that matter, informs the rapt reader:

26/vii/1962   Dear John, There is no doubt that I'm a xxxx of purest ray serene not to have answered the appeal of your 50th Anniversary Editor. I have such an allergy to these compilations that in spite of my esteem for you and wish to please, I can do nothing.

If you agree, and Larry permits, I'll write a few lines saying that I am prevented from saying what I should like to say but that I associate myself fully with all that L. D. says in your praise. I might add something to the effect that it shows what a godforsaken hole G.B. is that they can't make use of your undoubted talents. I'll cough up something and mail it to Larry for his information and necessary action.

By the way, he is going to Edinburgh for some parish meeting of publicans there. I suggest that there is no need for the sculptor to come to France. He can pick up Larry, who, I know will be glad to *sit for us both*. I enclose a passport snap of fizzog for sculptor's guidance.

38

The enclosed address was read out at the birthday feast in Moscow and then presented to me handsomely bound in blue Russia leather with my name and age inscribed on a silver plaque. Then my other Russian publisher (Grigori Vladikin of the State Publishing House of Literature) got up and made another eulogy, adding that he had just commissioned a translation of *Women Must Work*.

I can't begin to tell you how kind they were, nor what a seemingly very large public I have there—I was almost smothered in flowers, telegrams and letters, overwhelmed with visits, signings of innumerable copies of my books, and press conferences. Catha and I just had (contrary to my principles) to go on the Moscow radio and the Leningrad T.V.

No, I didn't celebrate on any likker. Warned in time I went as a T.T. on a régime, and did not touch anything all the time. Most fortunate. Catha said the vodka was terrific, the Georgian wine strong, and the Armenian brandy equal to the vodka. Ever yours Richard.

39

Sir William Haley

Carl Fallas introduced me to the early work of Richard Aldington in the nineteen-twenties. He and Aldington had known each other before 1914 and the picture of Aldington that Fallas gave me was enhanced by each successive poem, article, and novel by Aldington that I read. So much was this so that when I started to write on books under the name of Joseph Sell in *The Manchester Evening News* Aldington was the first author whose work I wrote about as a whole.

Aldington liked the piece. He told Fallas he was particularly pleased that I had realised *A Fool i' the Forest* had been a turning point in his life. The article appeared in 1933. We soon met and thereafter corresponded until war broke out. Aldington's letters were always welcome. He sent a stream of lively commentary from wherever he might be, the United States, Tobago, the English provinces, or anywhere else.

Then there was a very long silence. It was not broken

until I asked his permission to quote in the *Times* from one of his works. We took up the old links again—in a curious way we became more intimate although we were never again to meet.

In 1957 I felt detraction of Aldington was becoming so undiscriminating that his real achievements were being forgotten. I wrote an article to put what he had done into perspective. He was touched, and thanked me for "standing by an unpopular writer, who has some claims to being considered England's literary public enemy number one. It would be a kingly title but for the fact that it practically abolishes income." The correspondence ended with a card from Moscow, dated 4/7/62, telling me of the "quite unforgettable" welcome he had been given in Leningrad. "I find that, especially with the young, I rank as one of the most popular of English authors. Quite a change!"

The last three words tell one a great deal about Aldington. Although he sloughed off many illusions, and a number of his hates, he never altogether got rid of the chip on his shoulder. It antagonized some people. I myself never found that it got in the way of my liking for Aldington, his works, or what he stood for. Although the chip may have been ever-present it was not obtrusive. His anger at general stupidity was aimed at so many targets; his mind was so lively; his interests so wide; that he never had time to harp on anything. Aldington never bored.

About only one thing did I find him unduly defensive. That was his study of T. E. Lawrence. He never seemed to get rid of a need to justify his reading of *that* Lawrence. It was interesting that he remained emotionally unembroiled in the passions aroused by the other Lawrence, whose impact on him must have been much greater. He wrote and spoke about D. H. Lawrence with comparative detachment. He was indeed clearer eyed than many others who had known D. H. Lawrence about what was good and what was poor in Lawrence's works.

Maybe it was partly because Aldington's *Lawrence of Arabia* did him harm to the point of unfairness that he welcomed every scrap of justification. But even more, I believe, it was because of his exasperation that something he considered false should be so slow in becoming eroded. He sent me the paper-backed edition of the book because it contained in foot-notes testimony from a number of sources vindicating his views. He drew my attention to the pages on which they appeared and wrote on the title leaf (almost a cry of triumph?) "Magna est veritas, et prevalebit."

I don't want to give the feeling that Aldington was ever even a half-defeated man. He knew he had done good work. He had plenty of things to delight him in his later years. He was pleased with Gustave Cohen's translation, *Un Songe dans le Jardin de Luxembourg,* of his loveliest poem. He was delighted to receive recognition of his book on Mistral. He was gratified that "in the new history of English Literature" the Russians gave him a whole chapter. There was a warmth and happiness when he wrote about his daughter.

Warmth will remain the strongest memory I have of Aldington. A generous warmth, whether he was urging me to write about other authors he considered to be neglected, notably Norman Douglas; telling me, when a young man, how to forward my writing; declaring his "most humble admiration and love" for Professor Cohen, "a kind of war hero I admire"; or writing of his old friend Fallas, whose death occurred only three months before his own. Richard Aldington was a writer whose best works will be rediscovered for many years to come, and a man whose memory will not want affection so long as there is one of his friends left alive.

Alister Kershaw

Say what you like about British literary journalists, but you can't deny that they know what's required of them when a great writer dies. Team work! You need only look at the articles published after Richard Aldington's death: what marvellous co-ordination! The informed critic ("Richard Aldington's sudden death . . . will not have meant much to those in their forties and under"); the fair but forthright critic ("His talent was great but there was something missing"); the sheerly impudent ("Some books, such as . . . *Lawrence of Arabia,* are better forgotten"); the ridiculously inaccurate ("D. H. Lawrence, once a great friend, was attacked"); and, of course, the Deaf-Mutes (a couple of the most "serious" English papers didn't think it worthwhile mentioning Aldington's death at all). Team work!

And team work, what's more, even while the writer is still alive. Or very often. The effort devoted to poisoning Aldington's last years—awe-inspiring! Not that there was anything resembling a "plot," of course: when it's a question of harassing artists, there's never any need for conspiracy—the little men get down to it with spontaneous enthusiasm. Aldington, specifically, had been asking for trouble for years past—no denying that: with *Death of a Hero,* with *The Colonel's Daughter,* with *Very Heaven;* with those heterosexual poems of his; and then the formidable scholarship of the man—it was downright undemocratic.

Finally, with *Lawrence of Arabia* he went too far altogether. A scandal! To write the biography of a National Hero and to concentrate on the *facts!* No wonder that critics of the book—practically all of them, oddly enough, friends or eulogists of Lawrence—were outraged. No telling where this sort of thing might lead. Merciful Heavens! Supposing the fellow were to write a biography of . . .

One of Lawrence's infatuated hagiographers, I seem to remember, threatened Aldington with a horsewhipping! He might have found the task a bit tricky—Aldington was an unfashionably powerful physical specimen. The others, more cautiously, were satisfied merely to pronounce his excommunication—and here they had no trouble at all putting their edict into effect. The shrill upbraidings were succeeded by a virtually unbroken silence: with the exception of a generous article by Sir William Haley in the *Times,* Richard Aldington's name was scarcely ever mentioned in the English press from that time onwards, or, if mentioned at all, was invariably accompanied by some insolent attempt at belittlement. *La bonne affaire!* Publishers, notwithstanding their notoriously disinterested devotion to literature, don't publish authors who are so very much out of favour with the newspapers; newspapers don't write up authors who aren't published. A tacit gentlemen's agreement which lets everyone delicately off the hook. Everyone except Richard Aldington, of course.

It would have saddened his ill-wishers to see how little he allowed himself to be affected by this boycott. He accepted his circumstances as a logical consequence of his lifelong refusal to join the literary *lèche-cul* with their readiness—their servile eagerness—to "make useful contacts," to attend the appropriate parties, to simper winningly on television, to be photographed being kind to their dogs . . .

It was hopefully asserted from time to time that he had become "bitter" and "sour" as a result of the successful wrecking of his career. Some hope! Much he cared for the squeaks of a pack of sub-intellectuals in London pubs. It's amusing, too, that the little literary people, so repulsively jealous and mean-spirited themselves, should have affected to believe that Richard was "soured." He was, on the contrary, the least envy-ridden man I have ever encountered: at a time when he himself was going through the most difficult period of his existence, he was absolutely delighted by the success of Lawrence Durrell. His own situation was irrelevant when it was a question of saluting work that he felt to be good.

Again, some comfort was taken from the thought that his last years in a small cottage at Maison Sallé in the Berry must have been lonely. It is true that, for months on end, he would see nobody but his wine-growing neighbours and, especially, Maxime and Suzanne Gueneau and their charming children whose devotion to him was as deep and enduring as the hostility of the literary riffraff; but with his intense response to natural beauty and, above all, with his restlessly curious mind, he was incapable of the boredom which almost always underlies what people call loneliness. That astonishing range of interests! I remember when I first met him how eagerly he questioned me about Australia, at once revealing that he knew far more about my own country than I did myself. Later on, when I was staying with him in the south of France, I saw his passionate absorption in everything around him—everything from the wild life of the region to Provençal literature. So, in the Berry, he was fascinated to learn all about it—its history, its natural history, its architecture, its folklore.

He was immensely liked by his peasant neighbours. Not so much because he always produced some little present for their children's birthdays or because he was always ready to render any service he could but because, with their instinctive good breeding, they admired his lack of pretention, his natural dignity and his great courtesy. At a boisterous birthday celebration in a nearby farm house, Richard arrived towards the end of the meal to drink a glass of wine and everyone spontaneously stood up as he entered: a member of the French Academy would have been lucky to receive the same treatment from a roomful of tough French peasants . . .

Almost the only people he saw from outside were his daughter, Catherine, whenever she could get away from the university in Aix-en-Provence where she was studying, and my wife and myself with our small son (Richard's godson) whenever we could get away from Paris. These were always great occasions. Mostly Richard lived with an austerity which was wildly out of keeping with his temperament but which the triumphant destruction of his career made inevitable; but, whenever we came to stay, he always managed to arrange for superb dishes and astonishing wines ("Far too good for us, my dear boy, I know—but let's hope nobody finds out"). The only times, incidentally, when I ever heard him complain about his lack of money were when he was lamenting his inability to take us to some noteworthy local restaurant he'd heard of (not that there were many we didn't visit sooner or later) or to buy a gramophone for his godson (he eventually bought it) or to help out an old friend (he invariably found a way to help nonetheless).

During the last five years of his life, he hardly ever travelled outside the Berry—an occasional trip to see Catherine in the Midi, to Switzerland to visit H. D. or Bryher (who had reversed the usual process by *becoming* a friend, and an incredibly generous one, when Richard's circumstances were at their worst; the Australian writer, Geoffrey Dutton, was also among the handful of people who did something practical to help Richard at this time). But in 1962, the Soviet Writers' Union invited him and Catherine to visit the Soviet Union as their guests on the occasion of his seventieth birthday (an occasion duly celebrated in his native land by the customary dead silence) and, after considerable hesitation (he had reached a stage where he was reluctant to meet anyone new), he finally accepted.

A few days after his arrival in Moscow he wrote exuberantly—and with candid astonishment that it could actually be happening to such an outcast as himself—describing the fantastic welcome he received, not only from his official hosts but also from individual admirers of his work who wrote to him from all over the Union or came to his hotel and waited for hours to greet him or present some small gift. His letters grew more and more enthusiastic as time went on—the magnificence of the Kremlin collections, the splendour of Leningrad, the charm and distinction of the people he met—"The publishers I have visited," he wrote to me, "have been most affable and are really distinguished men who are highly cultivated (the complete antithesis of ———) . . . Interviews are published exactly and honestly and the reporters are civilized beings." It was an immense satisfaction to his friends to know that at long last he was being treated with the respect and consideration due to so great a writer—and so great a man.

Even his letters had not prepared me for my first sight of him on his return. As he got out of the car at the cottage in Maison Sallé where we were waiting for him, he looked younger and happier than I had ever seen him in the fifteen years since we had first met. It seemed impossible that he was seventy years of age and had just completed so long a journey.

Almost at once the cottage was transformed into the semblance of a Russian *datcha*. A huge poster of the Bolshoi Ballet was pinned up on the wall, a Russian record was placed on the gramophone, the samovar with which he had been presented for his birthday was set up in a place of honour and we settled down to the vodka and

caviar he had brought while he told us about the trip—
"Unbelievable, my dear boy. Of course, you'll say that
they'd got me mixed up with a *real* writer but I assure
you it wasn't so."

There were presents, inevitably—Richard could hardly
go outside the door without buying presents: a superbly
embroidered bag for my wife, marvellous Kazakhstan caps
for my small son, a magnificent *rubashka* for me. Neighbours came in to welcome him back and there were presents for them, too; scarves for the women, wooden dolls
for the children, little bottles of vodka for the men.

We came back to Paris some days after Richard's return
and my last sight of him was as he waved us good-bye
from the garden—handsome, unbelievably vigorous, full
of life. As we turned away, I said to my wife, "You know,
Richard will outlive us all." A little over a week later he
was dead.

Suzanne Gueneau telephoned to give me the appalling
news and I was at Maison Sallé early next morning, an
hour or two after Catherine, driving all night, arrived
from the Midi. Jacques Temple, most faithful of friends,
joined us there a little later.

On the morning of his death, Richard had driven as
usual into the nearby village of Sury-en-Vaux to collect his
mail. A few minutes after his return to the cottage, a
neighbour, Mme Rezard, saw him sitting in the garden
with his head in his hands and went over to see if he was
all right. Finding him ill, she called Maxime and Suzanne
Gueneau and they helped him into the house and telephoned to the doctor. All three remained with him until
the end. He was in great pain, they told me, but when-

50

ever they did anything for him he never failed to thank them each time. He died towards noon and Maxime and Suzanne Gueneau spent that night in the cottage, unable to bear the thought of his body being left alone.

He was buried in the cemetery of Sury-en-Vaux. His peasant neighbours were all present to salute his passing. And the London journalists were busily preparing to disparage him. *Da capo*.

Thomas MacGreevy

It was the very Irish setting of the *salon* at James Joyce's apartment in the Square Robiac near the Ecole Militaire that I first met that very English Englishman, Richard Aldington. The walls were hung with admirable contemporary portraits of Joyce and his family—one of them, that of Joyce's father, a *chef d'oeuvre*—by the Dublin painter Patrick Tuohy; and also with portraits of ancestors. For the religiously tormented Joyce was proud of the fact that his father's great-grandfather was own brother to the father of Daniel O'Connell, who won emancipation for the Catholics of Ireland—and, incidentally, the Catholics of England. The year I met Aldington in that room was probably 1928. For in the summer of 1927, during the intervals of taking tourists round Grenoble, of studying the history of art in Grenoble's lovely picture gallery and mooning to myself amongst the ghosts that haunt Grenoble and the country round Grenoble, the ghosts of Saint Bruno and Bayard, of Berlioz and Stendhal, I had com-

Thomas MacGreevy

pleted the first draft of my translation of Paul Valéry's *Introduction à la méthode de Léonard de Vinci.* In the intervening period I had been revising it, and looking round for a likely publisher for it. I had also been looking for encouragement about it and sometimes getting snubbed for my pains. A French "H.S.P." friend of Valéry's, wanting reassurance perhaps, as to my competence as a translator suggested that I should submit it for comment to an English cousin of his named Sturge Moore who counted for something in London literary circles. Despite encomiums by W. B. Yeats of Sturge Moore's poetic efforts I was no admirer of Sturge Moore. But to refuse to accept his cousin's proposal might give the impression that I was afraid, so I could only agree. And did. Moore read the translation—and spat! I may still have his very comminatory letter amongst my papers. But I was not discouraged. I had the self-confidence of youth.

That afternoon, Aldington had obviously come to pay a duty call on Joyce. There was no one else there and the atmosphere, though quite friendly, was relatively formal. With Joyce, I, myself, was used to being asked to give a hand with the correction of the proofs of what was then called *Work in Progress;* or to discussion on the symbolisms, derived from Vico (of whom I knew nothing except what I was told), underlying that work; or, more especially if Mrs. Joyce was present, to Irish reminiscence and fun. What I came upon now was more in the nature of an exchange of courtesies between Joyce and his visitor. Aldington did not stay long after I arrived. Before he left, however, he made a suggestion about my problem which Joyce endorsed and which I acted upon. It was to prove

53

rewarding. It was also to be the first of many helpfulnesses I experienced at the hands of Richard Aldington. The suggestion was that I should try my Valéry translation on a London publisher whose name, John Rodker, if I knew it at all, was not familiar. Aldington and Joyce both authorised me to use their names in writing to Rodker. Which I suppose I did. In any case Rodker agreed to publish the book and did so, in a small but handsome edition. It made neither my name nor my fortune but it pleased those I wanted it to please, and it was well received—so Valéry too was pleased.

I did not meet Aldington again for a considerable time. I did actually see him once but without realising that it was he. In between I had met Ernest Hemingway, also through Joyce. Physically, both Aldington and Hemingway were big men. They were about the same age. They had both published war novels—which were being talked about but which I had not read. I was still so little sure as to which of them was which that one night when I was dining with friends at the *Cochon-de-lait* and Aldington came in with a party I whispered to my friends that that was Ernest Hemingway. In succeeding months I met Hemingway again, not very frequently but sufficiently often to be able to identify him. So I knew that the other was Aldington. It was quite a time, however, and my Valéry translation had actually been published by Rodker, before I saw Aldington a third time. That was one night, when, crossing from the Boulevard du Montparnasse to the Val-de-Grâce on my way "home" to the Ecole Normale in the Rue d'Ulm, I recognised that a man sitting out on the Saint-Michel side of the Closerie des Lilas was

Richard Aldington. I went to him immediately and, re-introducing myself, told him that his suggestion about a publisher for my Valéry book had borne fruit and offered my thanks. He invited me to sit down and we talked for I suppose an hour. I gathered that he had been away but was back in Paris for a stay of some months. He was, I rather think, still at a hotel just then. But about then or shortly afterwards he rented an apartment in the Quarter, a few hundred yards from the Ecole Normale. There I saw him frequently over several months. And there we became friends.

Elsewhere I have discussed Richard Aldington's qualities as a writer. Here, it is as a friend I would write of him. Most of his values were not mine, yet as a friend I found him one of the most forbearing, most generous, most patient, most devoted and to crown all, most laughter-loving, friends I have ever had. In his personal relationships he, who could write so angrily of the collective shoddinesses that constitute what the Gospel calls "the world," was one of the most courteous of men. He enjoyed conversation and as a conversationalist was himself not only interesting but winning. His erudition was immense but it was the erudition of the humanist not of the pedant. One could disagree with his deductions and his asseverations, as I often did—in conversation as well as when I wrote about him—but never for a moment did disagreement cold the affectionately friendly spirit of our exchanges.

In theory Richard was basically the English free-lance Protestant anti-clerical that Irishmen take for granted. But he was not a Greek and Latin and Italian and French

55

scholar for nothing, so a priori he had some knowledge of the part played by the Church in the history of European civilisation. I was to discover in a little while that it was more than knowledge. For instance—he revered the memory of his father who had recently died and who, in his later years, had become a devout convert to Catholicism. Amongst his father's belongings that came to him there was a brand new suit of clothes which were too small for Richard and too big for me. Richard suggested that one of the men-servants at the Ecole Normale might be glad to have the suit. The *valet de chambre* who looked after the rooms on my corridor was about right for size. He assured me that he would be grateful for the gift. So I went off to fetch it. Then something unexpected happened. As he handed me the parcel, Richard, going all bashful, asked me whether I would tell the man that if he would be so good as to wear the suit going to Mass to begin with and, at Mass, say a prayer for the donor's father, the donor would be grateful. In time I was able to report back that when I passed on the request the valet had answered with full understanding and in good faith, "Mais certainement Monsieur, volontiers" and I can affirm that Richard was visibly pleased.

In this connection, an even stranger thing happened a year or so before Richard died. Thirty years before, he had repeated to me the hoary legend that Pope Leo the Tenth, Giovanni de'Medici, had once said, "God gave us the Papacy to enjoy. Let us enjoy it." I do not remember the occasion nor do I remember how I reacted. It now could be that I demurred. For I had read a good deal in von Pastor some years before and though I did not remember what the great historian had to say about Leo the Tenth, I did remember that he had had things to say about Alexander the Sixth which left a very different impression from that made by the things one read about the Borgia pontiff in English books. In addition, I had picked up the idea from W. B. Yeats that the last writer who should be trusted on the subject of the Roman emperors was Suetonius. Even in art history I knew that Vasari is not always reliable. And I still remember that when I finished reading a translation of Julius Caesar's *Gallic Wars* I decided for myself that I could not trust a single solitary thing that that gentleman had said about the Gauls. In short I knew that centuries of prestige do not necessarily prove the truth of propaganda. However that be, Richard, a year or so before he died, wrote to me from Rome, where he was studying in some library or other, that he had come on evidence which suggested that Pope Leo had never made the remark attributed to him. Clearly, since I do not think we ever referred to it again, Richard had it on his conscience that he had repeated it to me. Like most Englishmen he knew next to nothing about Irish history. He did not realise that since Ireland was starved into adopting the English language instead of its own, every Irish Catholic has had, sooner or later, to learn to treat English books as a priori one-sided and heretical and to trust nothing about his country or his religion that he reads in them. This, however, did not make it less touching that Richard wanted, after thirty years, to put himself right with me in the matter of poor Leo the Tenth.

Again, I remember that as he placed a generous offering in the collecting box beside the statue of Saint Anthony in the church of the "Santi Apostoli" in Rome with a special request for my "success" he mentioned that every favour he had ever asked at that shrine had been granted! (He had been going to Rome ever since about 1910 when he won a school or college money-prize and spent it on a first visit to the Eternal City.)

At both religious and secular levels, however, the dichotomies, the "contrarinesses," remained. Thus he clung to a paradoxically romantic idea of classical antiquity and when, in his writing, he attacked the contemporary establishment in his beloved England it was, I think because he saw England as falling short of the virtues attributed to *la cité antique*. As if, in antiquity or in the modern world, original sin had ever permitted the virtues of the *cité antique* to become anything more tangible than a philosopher's dream! But Richard did not believe in original sin. In his book on Lawrence of Arabia he writes of "the obsolescent idea of sin." No doubt, the disbelieving dons of his university days had taught him that the Greeks had no sense of sin, that sin was a Judeo-Christian concept bearing no relation to the *hubris-nemesis* alternative, with which specious argument some of them still go on expounding, despite evidence, plain enough to a less subtle-minded non-classics man like myself, that practically the whole corpus of Greek tragedy is primarily concerned with sin and the expiation of sin. The argumentations between Rich and myself were unending—yet, as I have said, uncloudedly friendly over all the years.

It was characteristic of Richard that, unlike many men, he took it for granted that his friends would like each other. Mostly, I imagine, his faith was justified. I have

particular reason to remember one instance—out of many
—with undying gratitude. At odd times over a decade of
years before I met Richard Aldington I had tried to write
poetry. A few poems had been published in periodicals.
But there were enough in my drawer to make a book and
I had met disappointment after disappointment when I
tried to publish them as a collection. A time came when
I retailed to Richard's friend and mine, A. S. Frere of
Heinemann's, the, for me, tragi-comic circumstances of
two of the disappointments. Frere's reaction was characteristically startling. He had not even seen the poems, but,
without hesitation and quite calmly, he said "I'll publish
them, Tom." And he did. And prevailed on the Viking
Press in New York to publish them too. The little book
set neither the Thames nor the Hudson on fire. For Frere's
sake and for the sake of Harold Ginsburg of the Viking
Press, I wished, and still wish, that it had more success.
(It goes without saying that to myself the immediate satisfaction of having it published was immense.) But Richard and another friend of Richard's came into the story too.
Frere asked Richard to write the blurb for the wrapper of
the book. Which Richard did in the most graceful and
sympathetic terms. And there was to be still more to it
than that. Earlier, Richard had introduced me, not casu-
ally but after some unexplained deliberation, to his friends,
Henry Church, a very wealthy American and his Bavarian
wife, Barbara, who lived in a beautiful eighteenth-century
house in a private park at Ville d'Avray. Henry wrote and
Barbara wrote. Henry published privately. Barbara did not
publish at all. They kept a rather small circle of friends,
scholars, men of letters, musicians, painters (they had

been amongst the first people to buy pictures by Georges Rouault). At a later date they founded the review *Mesures* but by that time I had left Paris. From the time Richard introduced me to them I was made to feel that I was *persona grata* at the beautiful house. Nor did they forget me as the years passed. They travelled a great deal but wherever they were, Paris or London, Berlin, Athens or New York, I would hear from them. Before Henry's death I saw them in London. After his death Barbara came with French friends to see me in Dublin, and when I was in New York in 1954 Wallace Stevens wrote to her from Hartford where he lived suggesting that she should give a luncheon party for me, with Miss Marianne Moore and himself as the only other guests. Which she did. There was a special reason why it had to be with Barbara that Wallace Stevens and I met. It was that Henry Church, who had died some years previously, was a friend of the famous poet as well as a friend of mine. He had given him my little book of poems to read. That reading had inspired Wallace Stevens to write his two moving and beautiful poems, *Our Stars Come from Ireland* and *The Westwardness of Everything*, the first with the epigraph, *Tom MacGreevy in America, Thinks of Himself as a Boy*. He had first sent me the poems in typescript. Then, in 1950, when his book, *The Auroras of Autumn*, in which they were included, was published, he sent me that. If my book had not had a popular success, these Wallace Stevens poems were so beautiful and the whole occurrence so unprecedented in my experience that I could not but feel overwhelmed—and, I hope, for Ireland if not for myself, permissibly proud. And it had all happened because, in some obscure way, Richard had sensed that if he brought me and the Churches together something worth-while, worth-while at a literary level, would come of it. I regard my modest share in the immortality of Wallace Stevens' two beautiful poems as the most *enduring* result of the many helpfulnesses I experienced at the hands of Richard Aldington. (To finish that story I may add that, as Wallace Stevens had never been to Europe and I had never been to America, some degree of risk attached to the prospect of our meeting that day at Barbara Church's. In the event it was, I think, a success. I know that, in retrospect, the others referred to the occasion as a happy one. I may also add that there had been a special reason for my meeting with Miss Moore too. But Richard does not come into that story.)

Returning more directly to the subject of Richard, I should explain that I had not come on any of the many books which I understand he published between the time I saw him prior to his departure for America at the beginning of 1939 and, maybe, the year 1960 when he sent me copies of his study of Mistral and his book on Lawrence of Arabia, the latter then already some years old and at the paperback edition stage. The Mistral is obviously of value as a work of literary *pietas* and also, perhaps, as a reminder to over "nordic" minded readers that all our major values, those of the Old Testament, those of the Gospel, those of the philosophy of Greece, come to us from the Mediterranean. Is there any culture, is there a great figure of any culture, that has not been profoundly influenced by them? As to the Lawrence book, I wonder whether, perhaps, Richard felt he had to write it as a duty to some regular officers of England—and of France—but, to me at least, the subject was not of much interest. I had, long ago, tried to read *Revolt in the Desert;* it did not hold me and I gave up without finishing it.

I had not met Richard for twenty-three years when, in June, 1962, we discovered that we were to be in Paris at the same time; I was returning from the Venice Biennale. Richard and his daughter were getting visas for a visit to Moscow where they were to be the guests of the Soviet literary establishment. With their friends, the Kershaws, they came to see me at my hotel in the Rue de Rivoli. I had understood that Richard's health, like my own, was not as good as it used to be. But he looked very well. In fact he looked as young and at least as debonair as he had looked a quarter of a century earlier. And he was as sympathetic as ever. We spent about an hour-and-a-half over a bottle of Krug, Richard and I reminiscing light-heartedly, the others letting us talk and joining in our laughter. Then they drove me to the Faubourg Saint-Honoré where I had business to attend to. It had been a happy reunion and as we said au revoir and they drove away, waving and smiling, leaving me on the pavement outside my picture gallery, I think we all hoped we should be meeting soon again.

A few weeks later, Richard, back in the quiet of the French countryside, wrote me a brief account of his Russian visit. He had not said whether there was a business side to the trip (it is, after all, well known that, vis-à-vis authors, the Russian publishing trade is as peculiar in its way as the Western publishing trade is peculiar in its way). But he was appreciative of his hosts' attentions and he was pleased that Soviet pressmen had not tried to make him talk to the Party Line in literature. To Richard, who liked the warmth of traditional Russian literature, the Party Line in literature was just more of what he would call "Communist tyranny and bunk." (He was not less contemptuous of the tycoonery that has been making itself felt in Western publishing.) Still he had been fêted, even if some of the fêting was probably because he had, in his writings, sometimes suggested that the England he loved could, in certain of its aspects, be less than an earthly paradise. We all know that under the Marxian dispensation, whether in Moscow or Peking, in Cuba or in Albania, there will be no original sin and that the earthly paradise will be—forever—just round the corner. The Richard Aldington of the nineteen-thirties used to dismiss Marxism as, to use his own words, "another of the panaceas." However, it was not the moment to remind him of that so I just wrote to say I was glad he had enjoyed the change to being a whiteheaded boy. Three mornings later, the morning my letter should have reached him, Richard died.

One evening long ago as we were standing in the Piazzale Michelangelo, with the sun going down over the splendour of Florence and an odd star beginning to show, Richard was trying to convince me of the glories of science as expounded by a celebrated man of whom I knew nothing but whom Richard had been reading, James Jeans. Recalling an earlier evening in Dublin when W. B. at his most endearingly oracular had said, "Science is a conspiracy," I asked Richard what was the good of science anyhow. I remember his answer, "It gets rid of fear." But I think it was with a reference to Pascal, who was a scientist and who was fearful, rather than to Saint John, that I countered. I do not know whether, since official Germany's extermination by scientific means of millions of Jews and uncounted Gentiles, and since the disgrace of Hiroshima, initiated by official America, approved by official England and official Russia, and, as a military measure, probably unparalleled in history since Jugurtha poisoned the wells, Richard would agree that science has created more fear than it has destroyed. I think he tended to believe, with his beloved Greeks, that the universe has a design and a purpose. I do not know, however, whether, before he died, he got even so far as to accept Saint John's affirmation that God is a spirit—Which has been seen by no man at any time but in Which we live and Which lives in us. Yet he was the kind of man of whom I dare to believe that, looking back over his seventy years of life, he would incline to the idea that Saint John probably knew better than the scientists how to deal with fear.

Morikimi Megata

I enjoyed the privilege of exchanging letters for ten years with one of the greatest figures in twentieth-century English literature. Richard Aldington wrote me thirty-four letters, while I sent him more than fifty. It was on 14 May 1952 that I first wrote to him when I was a student of Kyoto Imperial University, specialising in English literature and preparing a graduation thesis on D. H. Lawrence's *The Man Who Died*. I was not yet an ardent admirer or devoted reader of Aldington's work, though his fame as a poet and novelist was well known to me.

It was to Mr. Aldington as a friend and biographer of D. H. Lawrence that I took the liberty of writing. *Portrait of a Genius, but . . .* was then probably the only definitive and objective life of D. H. Lawrence existing and one which I read so many times that I felt as if I had known the author for years. In my letter I asked about Lawrence's use of the Isis-Osiris myth in *The Man Who Died*. Most unexpectedly a reply soon reached me from Montpellier,

France. I still vividly recollect how, startled and elated, I stood holding the letter in my hand.

Many thanks for your letter of the 14th inst. No, I don't think the Isis myth is the "nucleus" of *The Man Who Died*. *(May 25, 1952)*

So began a correspondence that was to continue for ten years. In his letter my Master corrected my misinterpretation of the story and advised me to get hold of all Lawrence's books, if I was intending a serious study of the novelist. I worked over my thesis until the end of the year and sent letters again and again, putting questions to my Master. Thus the origins of *The Border Line* and *Glad Ghosts* were explained, misdatings of some of Lawrence's undated letters in Huxley's collection and Frieda's *Not I, but the Wind* . . . corrected; Lawrence and his *Lady Chatterley's Lover* vindicated; my intellectualisations and rationalisations of Lawrence criticised.

The typescript of my thesis was finished in January, 1953. But for my Master's generous teachings through correspondence, it could never have taken any shape. In April, 1953, immediately after the graduation from Kyoto University, I moved from Kyoto to Kobe to teach English at Kobe City University of Foreign Studies.

> *Les Rosiers*
> *Ancien chemin de Castelnau*
> *Montpellier*
>
> *31 May 1953*

Dear Mr. Megata,

I think it is I who owed you a letter, though you graciously blame yourself. Believe me, I have thought much of you and should have written but for many moods of languour and discouragement. This year the Spring which is usually so lovely in southern Europe disappointed us all. Instead of warm rains followed by sun, we had weeks and weeks of cold with ground frost and hard cloudless skies. The earth hardened and dried to a depth of nearly two feet, the vines and all cultivated crops were late, and the wild flowers were far less abundant especially in the half-desert "causses" where they spring up suddenly after rain in the recesses of the limestone rocks. Then just as the fruit trees were in blossom, the cherries, the many kinds of peaches, the apricots, the plums, there came three days of brutal north-west wind (the "mistral") which shattered and drove the petals like sad snowstorms of lost hopes. . . . Indeed it is a disaster for these poor farmers who work so hard and are cheated by the town profiteers. . . .

So you are making the momentous change of moving from your home to the University at Kobe. It must be hard for you, and still harder for your parents who will try to hide their feelings of loss. But these changes are inevitable and we must try to accept them cheerfully. I look forward with dread to the time when my daughter, now so rapidly growing up, will have to leave me. Fortunately I like solitude. But I fear that for some time you may feel lonely in Kobe. You must remember you are young, that the young make friends easily, that you look towards the rising not the setting sun. . . .

Yes, yachting in the Mediterranean would be delicious. But, strange to say, it is a dangerous sea (you remember Shelley's death) and except for expert yachtsmen well acquainted with the conditions, nobody should venture very far on it even in summer. I have seen yachts actually wrecked on beaches crowded with summer bathers who tried in vain to help keep the ship off the rocks—so strong are the sudden winds and so peculiar the currents. Yet nothing pleases me more than to go out with the fishermen to catch the rock-fish and then to sail on to one of the

Isles d'Or (Port Cros for choice) and make a real bouillabaisse. It was the Provençal fishermen who taught me how delicious bêche-de-mer is. "Sea cucumber" the English call it. How absurd! And how delicious too are cuttle-fish when stuffed and cooked as Athenaeus describes in his Deipnosophists. Why do you not cheer your pupils by lecturing on Gastronomy in Literature?

With all good wishes,
Very sincerely yours,
Richard Aldington

Year by year, reading poetry in my class, English poetry became the speciality in my chosen field of study. "A serious study" of Lawrence given up, I still kept on writing about him until the end of April, 1962. The year 1961 brought me no letters from my Master who had moved to the Cher, though he graciously let me have a gift copy of *D. H. Lawrence* (Rowohlt, 1961) and a Christmas card.

I have been long in replying to your letters and hope you will forgive me. I came down here to spend the winter, in order to be near my daughter, but also (I hoped) to avoid the winter colds of the Cher and consequent sickness. Unfortunately I had a bad attack of bronchitis before Christmas, and recovered very slowly. You must remember that I am older than your father! I hope that will excuse my sending a mere card of greeting when you sent me that charming book of paintings, which delighted me and my daughter. (*February 22, 1962*)

In that letter my Master suggested that I should see his friend Jim MacDougall who was scheduled to spend a little time in Japan. By mischance I missed him when he visited Japan in April, 1962. I had just been admitted to the Graduate School of Arts and Sciences, Harvard, to work towards the degree of Ph.D. for the academic year 1962–63 in the field of English. I, with my wife and daughter, was staying for some time at my parents' home in Kyoto to consider the matter.

The very last letter of my Master's to me is a short one that reveals some of the impatience and irritation somehow common in older people.

It is indeed unfortunate that you missed Jim MacDougall, for I think he could certainly have advised you on the Harvard project and probably have been able to help. What a pity you did not arrange for your letters to be forwarded! (*April 24, 1962*)

It is indeed unfortunate that my Master's correspondence with me should have ended in this way. One morning towards the end of July, 1962, I read in the Japanese newspapers: "Richard Aldington, British novelist, died near Léré, mid-France, on July 27. . . ." I felt as if the skies had fallen.

In the course of our correspondence, I sent him sword guards, some books of Japanese art and literature as tokens of gratitude and seasonal greetings. He never failed to make returns. He was generous enough to send me gorgeous Christmas cards, his books, and even transfer to me a sum of 100,000 yen from his blocked account. In every letter he wrote to me he wished my wife and myself all happiness, and he often added his daughter's name to his own signature. He sent us warm congratulations on our

69

marriage and on the birth of our daughter. He wrote at once to ask after us when he read the news of the typhoons that had struck Japan. He was a gentleman, so warm, so tender-hearted.

During the last ten years, I read his novels, poems, and studies—those available to me. I like *Death of a Hero* and *All Men are Enemies* very much, the former with its savage anger and bitter poignancy and the latter with its maturity and finish as a beautiful *Bildungsroman*. How I love his poems, some with Greek clarity and simplicity, some with bitter poignant realism, and some with beautiful dreams and vivid sensuous images! How I wish in vain that I had done some serious study of his poetry with my Master's help while he was still alive! So far as I know, no serious full-length study of him has yet been done in Japan, though all those concerned with English literature have paid keen attention and given high praise to this many-sided man of letters. The trouble is that of the many books he has published, those available to us are very few. I regret that my own little article on Richard Aldington which I contributed to my university journal can hardly be said to have done him justice. His books, from *Death of a Hero, All Men are Enemies, Soft Answers* down to *D. H. Lawrence* and *Eliot and Yeats,* are well read, so far as they are obtainable. It is pleasant to be able to record that, here, in Japan, *Death of a Hero* and *All Men are Enemies* (Part I only) have recently been published, though in a very abridged form, as a textbook for university students.

In his letters, Aldington was usually gay, happy and enjoying life, though he often complained of ill health,

sometimes attacked the persons he disliked, voiced his indignation at the evils of the time. He wrote about his life
and work, observations of nature and the turns of seasons,
descriptions of various scenes in France, Japanese art and
literature, Greek and Latin classics, Christianity, various
aspects of and figures in English, French and Italian literature.

I like to fancy that my Master wrote me so many
letters because of his youthful yearning for the dream-land
of mystery and beauty depicted by Hokusai and Hearn.
His interest in Japan was very keen; his knowledge of pre-
war Japan accurate; but he did not show an understanding
of or sympathy with the changes that have taken place
since the end of the war in 1945.

There is a passing reference to the celebration of his
61st birthday (*kanreki*).

With this I am sending you a snapshot of myself as a soldier
taken in 1916 during the first world war. I would rather you
think of me as a young man than as the old man I am now.
I read somewhere (in a European book on Japan) that in the
old days when a Japanese reached the age of sixty he put on a
red robe and red cap, and said he had reached his second childhood. Alas! I must buy myself a red cap. (*October 18, 1952*)

He sent us warm congratulations on our marriage by
transcribing a Japanese *waka* poem by Atsutada.

First allow me to send my warmest congratulations on your
marriage. What can I wish you both? I copy out the transcription of a poem of Atsutada which I think very beautiful and
feel sure will be true of you both:

71

"Aimite no
   nochi no kokoro ni
kurabureba
   mukashi wa mono wo
   omowazari keri!"

I wonder if the transcription into European lettering still leaves it comprehensible, or if it is completely garbled? But in any case I wish you both all happiness. (*March 5, 1958*)

Twice or thrice he speaks of his "small collection of Japanese colour prints."

But there are many things in Japan which are hard for us to understand. I have a small collection of Japanese colour prints, quite ordinary ones—Hokusai, Hiroshige, Toyokuni, and so forth —and their beautiful bright colours seem arranged with such perfect taste and give so much pleasure in our drab commercial world. Yet I learn that in the Imperial Family and among the great aristocrats all this colour is thought bad taste, and only the severest black and white and unstained woods are permitted. Now, in Europe it was the old kingly and aristocratic world which abounded in beautiful colour, and it was the triumph of the bourgeoisie which imposed black and white on us, as the triumph of the proletariat has imposed a sort of dirty drab khaki mis-named "utility." Only now is colour coming back into women's dresses and men's shirts and ties. And my colour prints, I am told, are often theatrical scenes showing some well-known actor, sold in the streets for a few pence. It is strange. (*June 14, 1952*)

I remember writing a long letter in reply to this, discussing colour and class in Japan. Again my Master speaks of the *Ukiyoe* prints, from which "much is still to be learned":

72

As a matter of fact, I have only about 150, mostly Hiroshige, Toyokuni, Kuniyoshi, with odd specimens of Hokusai, Utamaro, Kiyonaga and others less renowned. They are a great pleasure to me, and I believe that European artists still have lessons to learn from them. I need not tell you how much such artists as Whistler and Matisse owe to these prints. Artistically their influence is less marked now, but I think they show how artists to-day might still find means of reaching a public whom they have estranged by too much professionalism, too disdainful an attitude and a complete neglect of themes which might interest those who are not professional artists. (*September 10, 1952*)

He admires Waley's translations of the *Tale of Genji* and Chinese poems (November 17, 1953) and speaks of the melancholy of the autumn months for ladies living in solitude as recorded by the Lady of Murasaki (October 18, 1952). There is no reference to the Japanese *Haiku* poems in his letters to me, but that he has had some knowledge of them is indisputable. We may sense in some of his earlier poems the influence of the *Haiku*. I do not think, however, that Japanese art and literature influenced him much; whatever strong attraction he might have found in the Japanese "culture and traditions, matured through so many centuries of civilisation":

What is so attractive (to me) in the ancient Japanese work is the mingling of exquisite aristocratic breeding with artistic sensibility and creativeness. Something of the kind existed in ancient Egypt where the Pharaoh also was Son of the Sun—Ra. In Greece, between Homer and the triumph of Christianity (Judaism), there were also epochs of real aesthetic distinction, though the Spartans were base militarists, and the Athenians sometimes rather vulgar. And then it was lost for nearly 1,000 years, to be

73

revived by the Italians in the 15th century, spread through Europe, and lost again by the French Revolution. It was the English who substituted puritanism, money-getting, predatory trade and machinism for Life and Art. And so we are where we are, and between America and Russia I can't see that Civilisation can revive for a very long time, if ever. But there! old men are always gloomy, translating their own decrepitude to the times. All may seem roseate in the future to you. (*April 6, 1954*)

My Master recalls the far-off days when he was an English schoolboy.

How well I remember the Russo-Japanese war of 1904 (was it?) and how we English schoolboys wore little Japanese flags in our button-holes and prayed for Japanese victory! Soon after I began reading Lafcadio Hearn. (*May 16, 1959*)

My Master's feelings toward Japan must have been the yearning for the island-empire of beauty and mystery which had been so long isolated in the Far East.

It is quite possible that we European writers and artists tend to idealise Japan, simply because in its art and poetry and in the carefully selected impression given by such writers as Lafcadio Hearn, we seem to find in Japan the dream-country of beauty and distinction and good manners and religious tolerance of which we dreamed in youth and no longer dare hope for. But no race, however pure and disciplined, can long endure the degrading influence of modern industrialism and Americanism. It was an evil day when the barbarians of the West in their warships shattered the calm isolation of that beautiful world. We should have come humbly to learn instead of arrogantly to conquer. Please remember that we English are not Americans. We do not believe in unlicensed democracy, chewing gum and coca

Richard Aldington as a youth in 1905. Courtesy of Mrs. Margery Gilbert.

The poets visit Newbuildings, Sunday, January 18, 1914. Richard Aldington is the second from the right. With him are Victor Plarr, Sturge Moore, W. B. Yeats, Wilfrid Scawen Blunt, Ezra Pound, and F. S. Flint. Courtesy of the Rt. Hon. the Earl of Lytton, O.B.E.

Richard Aldington, looking smart in his uniform, is shown in 1917 as an officer during World War I. Courtesy of Lt. Col. H. F. L. Castle.

An informal shot of Richard Aldington on the island of Port Cros, southeast of Toulon, in 1929. Courtesy of Mrs. Margery Gilbert.

Alister Kershaw and Richard Aldington on a picnic in the country-side in Provence in 1947. Provence was Richard Aldington's home for many years. Courtesy of Adrian Lawlor.

Richard Aldington stands with his daughter Catherine in this snap-shot taken in 1955 at Montpellier. Courtesy of F.-J. Temple.

This casual photograph taken in 1959 includes Richard Aldington, Lawrence Durrell, Henry Miller, and Jacques Temple. Courtesy of F.-J. Temple.

Richard Aldington was honored by the Writers' Union of the U.S.S.R. on the occasion of his seventieth birthday in 1962. This photograph, one of the last taken of Aldington, was taken on that trip to Moscow. Courtesy of the Literary Gazette, Moscow.

cola, and though the war has for ever shattered our power and made us poor, we still believe in loyalty to the Queen and in a code of manners. Again, a poor England has much to learn from the poor island-empire of the East—I mean poor in comparison with American wastefulness. In England poverty is still thought vulgar—we must try to make it the supreme elegance. (*September 10, 1952*)

It is clear that what my Master cares for is the ancient Japan before the Meiji Restoration (1868) that introduced modernisation and westernisation, or at least the prewar Japan that was still the great Empire in the Far East, with all her pomp and power.

In spite of the excellence of modern Japanese paintings, I hope Japan will not become too modernised. Your ancient culture and traditions, matured through so many centuries of civilisation, are far too precious to be lost. (*February 22, 1962*)

Again:

I do not believe that Japan can or should become a "democracy" in the American or even Western European sense. (*October 18, 1952*)

And again:

"Democracy" leads always to demagogy, and to anarchy, and thence to tyranny—it is all explained by Aristotle and Plato—2000 years ago. But I am grieved that this should happen in a truly aristocratic country like Japan. (*December 12, 1959*)

I was greatly pleased recently to learn that in old Japan there were not only anniversary feasts for children, but also for very

75

old people, and that in some cases even the Emperor deigned to send congratulations and a small present—or it was sent in H.I.M.'s name. It is rather different over here now, where the older I get the more disagreeable are the demands for taxes I receive! On my 65th birthday I received congratulatory telegrams from no government but the Russian! (*March 13, 1959*)

To my Master the Emperor was still "the Sacred Person" (October 1, 1959), though the Emperor himself denied his divinity in the New Year Rescript in 1946. He ironically asks,

Why has His Imperial Majesty's Government ceased to use the 16 petalled chrysanthemum as an emblem on all stamps? Does this mean a new era? And a new emblem? I hope it will not be a packet of chewing gum or a newspaper. (*April 6, 1954*)

One of the ideals cherished by the human race is surely some day to reach a synthesis of the two different cultures of the East and the West. Aldington was eager that there should be more opportunities for the West to know about the East and vice versa.

What we sadly need in Europe is an organised set of translations of the great classics of the Orient and translations of new books of interest. Such things do exist, but they are in some case limited to religious and philosophical works, e.g. Max Müller's *Wisdom of the East;* in other cases they are difficult to obtain, as the publications of the Asiatic Society; and often the translations are miserably inadequate. But with the untold sums which are lavished on armaments and the ceaseless plotting and planning, nothing is done about literature. (*November 17, 1953*)

76

Morikimi Megata

My Master made his brilliant début in letters as an experimentalist in poetry. But one cannot forget that he was a man of letters deeply rooted in the tradition of European culture. His tremendously deep and wide scholarship is revealed by his translations from Greek, Latin, French, and Italian and his admirable studies in French literature. He seemed happy and pleased to speak to me out of his immense scholarship. Not long after the beginning of our correspondence he offered me a list of major readings from Homer down to the Authorised Version. (October 24, 1953) Born and bred in the long tradition of European literature, he undoubtedly added to it something new, valuable, and again, permanent.

England has seen so many exiles: Lord Byron, P. B. Shelley, R. L. Stevenson, D. H. Lawrence, and James Joyce. My Master too died an exile. If Matthew Arnold's criticism of her was right, England, with her provinciality and philistinism, may have virtually expelled them. But England is also the country where those rebels have triumphed at last.

I do not know what judgment will be passed upon my Master by generations yet to come in his native land. But here is the one sure thing that I know. The image of my Master, Richard Aldington the man, with all his warmth, goodwill, generosity, and tenderness, his love of nature, human beings, and the cultural heritage of the human race, is still vividly alive in my heart, my wife's and parents'.

I offer up prayers for him from the dream-land of mystery and beauty that Hokusai and Hearn depicted.

Henry Miller

He was not the sort of man I had expected to meet. That was my first impression. He was bigger, bolder, kinder, more sympathetic—and far less British—than I had pictured him in my mind. *A good human being,* I thought to myself. More like some fine breed of dog than a literary creature. Something in his eyes which spelled sadness—not human sadness, but the sadness of the animal which knows not why it is sad. Or, as if at some time or other he had experienced a profound betrayal.

I had the feeling, though I made no mention of it, that he was not long for this earth. Not that he looked ill—on the contrary, he seemed like a mighty oak of a man—but rather, that he gave the impression of weariness, weariness due to combatting human stupidity, meanness, and so on. As if he had given up the fight.

And then, later in the day, after we had all had dinner together—the Temples, the Durrells, my wife and I—to my surprise he waxed jovial. He laughed, drank, told stories—as a man might who had been deprived of human companionship for many moons.

It is unfortunate that we so often happen upon our companions-in-writing late in life. Even had he not died I doubt that I should ever have run into him again. There are people we are destined to meet just once in a lifetime.

Soon we will meet again—in that other world where time and space are meaningless. Then we will really get acquainted.

Harry T. Moore

The morning train from the Gare de Lyon took some two hours to reach Cosne, on the Nivernais side of the Loire. During the last part of my journey the famous river had flashed in and out of view beyond its poplars. Richard Aldington and I hadn't arranged any signals of recognition for our meeting at Cosne: he could certainly be identified from his photographs, and presumably he'd know a visiting American. Sure enough, there he was at Cosne, his face a little heavier and older than the pictures, his moustache greying. His eyes were bright and fine, with the look of a man who relished life.

His recent books on Norman Douglas and on Lawrence of Arabia had been harshly attacked in the British press, and he had been called an embittered and frustrated man. But the Richard Aldington I met on that August day of 1958 at Cosne and on several later visits there in the next few years, and with whom I was to exchange many letters in that period, was not at all frustrated and embittered.

Certainly he was critical of some phases of civilization, a mark of intelligence and sensitivity, but he expressed himself without dogmatic frenzy, and he showed no corroding grievance. His wit was sharp, his tone cheerful.

After our meeting at the station, we went in his little car to a restaurant where we had fish with an excellent Pouilly-Fumé. His repertory of pungent stories was extensive. There were many about D. H. Lawrence, who was the object of my visit because I was editing his *Collected Letters* (and was in Europe on a Guggenheim Fellowship). Richard brought Lawrence and other members of the dramatis personae of modern literature brightly to life. He neatly projected the speech and postures of Ezra Pound, whom I had met, and he imitated the manner of the earlier Ford Madox Ford, of the Hueffer days. He was particularly amusing when he mimicked Ford and Pound competing for domination at one of Wilfrid Scawen Blunt's birthday celebrations; there is a photograph of this, with Richard looking very young; he said it was Blunt's seventieth anniversary, but that would have been in 1910, before Richard was associating with Pound and Ford; it was probably the seventy-fifth, in 1915 but, whatever the date, Richard was very funny "doing" the party. I want to make it clear that none of this was done with malice; it was all mischievous fun.

After lunch we crossed the "ruban lumière" into the Berry, where Richard lived. On the way to his village we stopped at Sancerre, a hill-town with a round stone medieval tower. At a pottery shop I bought a souvenir I still have, a small glazed-clay brown ram with curled horns.

It's a rather powerful little whistle, apparently used by shepherds.

We drove on tangled roads among wheatfields and vineyards. Richard's cottage at Sury-en-Vaux was known locally as Chez Alister Kershaw. Alister Kershaw is a bearded young Australian married to an English girl with flashing black eyes. The Kershaws, who are devoutly Gallicized, make their headquarters in an apartment in the working-class quarter of Paris, which they think is paradise. Richard was living in their country home.

Through that first afternoon we sat talking in a book-walled room that looked out on what the Duke of Burgundy in *King Henry V* calls "this best garden of the world, / Our fertile France." Richard Aldington recalled that view in a letter a few months later (23 October 1958):

I wish you could manage to spend a little longer time here with Mrs. Moore, because there is so much in the neighbourhood of great interest. A primitive society still living in pre-Revolution conditions. Most interesting. I must try to find you the reproductions of the Duc de Berry's Book of Hours—the same scenes are still visible from the cottage windows. Now we have what is called a "strong government" it will be destroyed no doubt.

He spoke of this view again (7 December 1959) after he had been visiting his ex-wife in Geneva (or was it Paris?):

When I was in H. D.'s apartment last week I saw on her table the Belle Livre des Heures du Duc de Berry from the N.Y. Cloisters. I didn't know about that one. You must have thought me nuts to say I could witness the same scenes from my windows here. But there is also (at Chantilly) the Très Riche Livre [sic] des Heures du Duc de Berry, a series of farm scenes from the 15th century which still go on—the man ploughing with a horse, the people making hay with pitchforks, bringing in faggots for the winter, old women or children driving out and watching cows and goats, etc. The hay is now cut by machinery, and they have some tractors for ploughing, also reapers and binders, and threshing machines: but the rest is still the immemorial usage. The women grow the vegetables, do the washing in the pool just up the road, and hold all the money. Quite Lawrentian.

I can't distinguish what we said on that first afternoon from our conversations on later visits, so will try to telescope my memories of them, often drawing upon Richard's letters. We didn't always sit talking in Maison Sallé, but sometimes dashed across the country in that tiny car. We stopped to go into shadowed, cool, old churches, we drank champagne at sidewalk cafés in the towns, and we went to places connected with Balzac and George Sand. We drove south of Bourges to Epineuille-Fleuriel, where Alain Fournier had grown up, and to nearby Meaulnes which had given him the name for his novel, *Le Grand Meaulnes,* whose pages so marvelously evoke that countryside.

We discussed a current author Richard intensely admired, Lawrence Durrell, of whom he subsequently wrote (24 January 1959):

Although he is different from DHL, I find something of the same excitement in LD—I mean that his intense awareness of the living world of Alexandria and its people, plus his amazing literary (innate) skill in giving me what he has seen and experienced, remind me of the first contacts with DHL's work.

(Of course the puritan [Lawrence] would have been outraged by
LD, and have predicted madness and death in a year!)

This last refers to Lawrence's warning to Richard when
he read the first part of the manuscript of *Death of a
Hero:* "If you publish this, you'll lose what reputation
you have—you're plainly on the way to an insane asylum."
That conversation had taken place in the autumn of 1928,
barely a year before Lawrence's death; he and Frieda were
with Aldington, Dorothy Yorke, and Brigit Patmore at
the Vigie (observation fortress) on the island of Port Cros,
southeast of Toulon. The whole story of that wild visit
hasn't been fully told, but Lawrence's letters and a few
other sources give some hint of what happened. While at
Port Cros, Lawrence read *Point Counter Point* by his
friend Aldous Huxley, to whom he wrote: "And if murder, suicide, rape, is what you thrill to, and nothing else,
then it's your destiny—you can't change it *mentally.*"
Richard Aldington, Lawrence added, was just as bad.

Lawrence's temper or health hadn't been improved by
the arrival at Port Cros of a batch of reviews of *Lady
Chatterley's Lover* which generally indicated that its
author was an inhabitant of the sewers. Brigit Patmore,
in her lively but necessarily incomplete memoir ("A dis-
cord had developed on the island"), portrays Lawrence as
ill but jovial at Port Cros. Lawrence later told a friend,
speaking of Richard: "But since the Vigie I don't write
to him—that's a long story." And it can't all be told yet,
though Richard in conversation added to my knowledge
of the episode, and at least one bit, now in print, can be
mentioned here. In his autobiography, *Life for Life's Sake,*

Richard noted that Frieda had arrived late from Florence, taking a detour via Trieste. Richard told me that in this case Trieste meant tryst. With his permission this bit of information was included in the revised (Penguin and Grove Press) edition of my Lawrence biography, *The Intelligent Heart,* in 1960, along with Richard's further point that, in the last five years of Lawrence's life (1925–30), Frieda used to go about complaining that he had become impotent—an interesting and significant footnote to the Lawrence-Frieda relationship and to *Lady Chatterley's Lover.* Lawrence in his letters from Port Cros mentions that he had caught a cold from Frieda. Richard's imitation of him, complaining about that "vile Italian cold" imported by Frieda was extremely funny, rendered in the Midlands accent Lawrence had never quite shaken off.

Lawrence, Richard wrote (in that 24 January 1959 letter) lacked Durrell's "sense of comedy farce"; "he had satirical wit galore, but not just sheer laughter." After recommending Durrell's three Alexandria novels ("a fourth, completing the quartet, is now being written in a Languedoc mazet"), he suggested: "Try also *Esprit de Corps* and *Stiff Upper Lip,* the dip. corps comedy-farces. (LD was many years a Foreign Office press officer.) Almost his greatest friend is Henry Miller, who after reading the start of *Esprit de Corps,* wrote: 'Don't do it again, even for money.'"

Durrell was one of Aldington's few recent enthusiasms. He deplored the growing admiration for Henry James, to me one of the greatest of writers; to Richard he was always, with a chuckle, "Henrietta James." And he decried what he considered to be the domination, in British literary

85

circles, of the sexual left. On being reminded that he had edited and provided a friendly preface for an Oscar Wilde anthology and that he had written favorably of a living author whose proclivities are widely advertised, Richard smiled and said, "Ah, but they're good fairies!"

Richard's 1954 book about Norman Douglas and Pino Orioli, rather unfortunately named *Pinorman*, stressed some elements about Douglas' sexual life that were already well known, indeed mentioned by him in his autobiography, *Looking Back*. Richard criticized Douglas's attack on Lawrence in relation to Maurice Magnus, whom Lawrence wrote of as a sponger; but Richard had a certain admiration for Douglas as a bluff old rogue. As for the 1955 book on the other Lawrence, "of Arabia," he not only shook the Establishment by portraying that mysterious figure as both illegitimate and homosexual, ideas long current outside of print, but he also outraged Lawrence's hero-worshippers by suggesting that their idol was a fraud. In regard to protests against that last idea, Richard told me at Sury that he had plenty of proof, besides the documentation in the book itself, and in our correspondence he referred (on 16 February 1959) to "personal letters from generals, staff officers, fighting officers and political officers, English and French in the Mid East, which back me and expose the interested reviewers." He noted later (14 October 1961):

The Sunday Times has been publishing parts of Anthony Nutting's attempt to revive the "heroic" TELawrence, in which he virtually accused me of having concocted a letter from Lawrence to Charlotte [Mrs. Bernard] Shaw in which the "hero" admits he had not told the complete truth about the Deraa episode, and confesses that he yielded to the homosexual Bey to avoid further beating-up. I didn't see this [article], but when I received a marked copy I wrote a moderate letter stating that if the Lawrence letter is not in the Brit Mus Library then it has been removed, and that I have a copy of it. Meanwhile, however, someone wrote in and quoted the original (which of course is still in the B.M.) only a few days before. They used (inconspicuously) the letter with the quote, refused [Stanley] Weintraub's letter, and neither used mine nor acknowledged nor apologised. Such is the freedom of the press under the British Establishment in 1961—a sad indication of how England has fallen to being the sick man of Europe. . . . TEL wrote Charlotte Shaw that the main reason for joining the RAF as an A/C 2 was to avoid his terrible old Mom, who wanted to atone for her "sin" by imposing herself on him as his housekeeper and forcing him into her particular sect of virulent Calvinism. You understand, of course, that the Lawrence Trust refused permission for me to quote these letters in my book, and I had to give as my opinion what Lawrence himself had confessed in writing. This Nutting article is the first reference to those letters by one of the Lawrence Bureau, and that in a foolish attempt to insinuate that they don't exist. They have never answered me, because they can't—everything I said is documented and the refs carefully given.

Earlier, I had asked Richard if I could use in D. H. Lawrence's *Collected Letters* some of the outrageous things which Lawrence had said about him; I was trying to avoid all the blanks that had marred the Huxley edition, printed in 1932, when the Lawrence battles were closer in time and, in any event, regarded less as honorable engagements than they were later, when Lawrence was at last widely recognized as a writer of magnitude. I told Richard about one of Lawrence's statements concerning H. D., a particularly nasty one even with the passing of the years. Richard wrote (23 October 1959):

En principe, I don't mind anything in DHL's letters about me being published. After the onslaughts over Douglas and T. E. Lawrence I ought to have the fabled hippo's hide by now. (Beware of offending the International Order of Pederasts!) But H. D. is terribly sensitive about such things, and the Lawrences had the bad habit of gossiping by word of mouth and letter about their friends, without really knowing the facts. . . . All Lorenzo's surmises and censures of H. D. are poppycock—they had a row about something, god knows what.

The omitted passage, indicated by dots, in the preceding quotation is information that was given "in complete confidence to yourself and Mrs. Moore," and although both Richard Aldington and H. D. are now dead and beyond harm from its being quoted, I still feel too confidentially bound in about the matter to include the passage just now. Richard was always sensitive on the score of his former wife, and continually felt protective toward her. In March 1959 he was pleased to learn that she was to receive a Brandeis University Gold Medal, but wondered just what that was ("She ought to have had the Pulitzer long ago"); the Brandeis award must carry some prestige, he felt, for H. D. reported that her friend Norman Holmes Pearson of Yale University was pleased over it, and this was good. Later (6 April 1960), when H. D. was about to go to the States for the ceremony, Richard saw her [in Geneva!] and said she "looked better than during the winter months. The lovely view across the lake from

her windows was now visible, and not veiled in Swiss fog."
But she was "still very nervy," and he wondered whether
"this visiting fireman trip home is altogether good for
her." Her novel, *Bid Me To Live*, written years before,
was about to be published:

This morning I got a cable from London asking me to try to
get Hilda's novel for Chapman and Hall. I expect Pearson has
already sold British rights, but I sent the cable on to Bryher
[in Geneva?]. Hilda gets so nervous about such things, it is
better not to trouble her with them. She—H. D.—very much
wanted me to come with her to US on this affair. Can't you
see the headlines: "Aged Poets Reconciled—Living Incog. in
5th Av. Hotel" (that was her bright idea)—and what would
my present legal wife, Catha's mother, say?

Ezra Pound, the frequent subject of our talks and letters, was mentioned in a postscript (20 October 1959):

There is a little sheet called Agenda just in from a south London suburb—Battersea. It consists of 4 pages, mostly by "Noel
Stock," a most obvious pseudonym for Ezra. [Noel Stock is
actually an Australian poet, a collaborator of Ezra Pound.] The
same old weary fascist propaganda—war started by wicked England and wicked FDR against innocent Schicklgruber and saintly
Musso. Gives you a pain. Why can't he drop it all, accept defeat
on that front, and go back to poetry?

The same letter also expresses regret that the British
fascist Sir Oswald Mosley wasn't willing to drop his political activity. Contrary to a widespread belief, Richard Aldington wasn't antidemocratic; in our talks he was often
critical of the politics of democratic states, yet he chose

to live in countries whose citizens still had some choice on their ballots. He took a close interest in elections (20 July 1960):

I think that Stevenson's failure to secure the presidency 8 years ago was a calamity. If he had been in the White House instead of Ike, I think the world would be happier and safer. Don't care much about an Irish Roman Catholic, almost bound to carry out a Vatican policy. But surely better than Nixon with another Dulles in the background. The whole US and Allied policy needs revision, and they must begin by abandoning lost causes, and recognise the Red chinks, bastards though they may be.

In a subsequent letter, he spoke more friendlily of President Kennedy for his rôle in the release of Francis Gary Powers from imprisonment in Soviet Russia.

Early in the next year, Richard wrote (4 April 1960):

It will be good to see you and your wife on the 13th or 15th July—we can make arrangements later. Remember that those days are very crowded on the French railways—paid holidays starting. So it would be wise to reserve seats ahead through American Express.

He added, on 9 April, "I won't importune you, knowing you pressed for time you'll be in Europe, but if you can manage to run down here I'll be delighted to see you, and to have your news." In the 4 April letter, he said, concerning D. H. Lawrence's troubles during the first war:

I agree with you wholly in thinking that fat Ford's account of L. and Frieda and their pro-Germanism [at Greatham in 1915] is sheer romancing—that fellow wouldn't have recognised Truth if he'd met her. BUT, L. had talked indiscreetly to others, he had German relatives, he had been living in Germany, he had a German wife. I think we've overlooked the damage of the association with Russell, who was a prominent member of the No Conscription society (fellowship?), was fined 100 pounds in 1915 for writing a pacifist tract and eventually jailed for 6 months in 1918 for writing that the American army had been sent to do in England what it did in its own country—put down strikes! (I remember thinking of that in 1930 when I stopped my car near Château Thierry to take off my cap to the monument to the U.S. war dead.)

I mentioned an idea which had recently been presented by David Garnett in a lecture at Southern Illinois University; he believes that Ford warned the government in 1915 that the Lawrences were pro-German, and that all their troubles during the rest of the war stemmed from Ford's report. Richard commented (5 May 1960):

I'd hate to think that fat Fordie had been so goddam mean as to put in an unfavourable official report on the civisme of Lorenzo and Frieda. If he did, what a bastard. Of course, he needed to whitewash himself—he looked as much a Hun as Hindenburg—and, it is true, that pre-war he was friends with the Minister of Education, C. F. G. Masterman. (My belief is that Masterman was dropped from the Cabinet when the coalition was formed in 1915.) I was Ford's secretary while he was writing or dictating that anti-German book, When Blood is Their Argument, and I'm pretty sure Masterman got him the job in the Foreign Office. I got so fed up with Ford I quit, and Alec Randall took over, finished the second book (I had begun with F.) and got the job at the F.O. I should have had. What a mercy—Alec became an ambassador and a K.C.M.G.!

In a later letter (20 July 1960), sent to Nice, he mentions another projected trip to Sury: "The 11th August is perfectly all right for our visit, so far as I know. These holiday times are so awful in Europe that I lie low from mid-July to mid-September, and move about before and after" (and he was still at Sury when I went down there again the second week of August). In the same letter to Nice, warning me about a proposed journey for the purpose of looking up sites connected with Rilke and Kafka, he again demonstrated how anti-Red hysteria had lowered American prestige abroad: "If you do go to Prague, better ask the US Embassy about it first. With all the fuss going on, the stamping of the Czech visa on your passport might attract attention. What a pack of fools they are—squabbling about nothing." A friend of a friend at the U.S. Embassy was consulted, and of course there was no trouble over a literary visit to Prague—except from the Czechs, who kept imposing the kind of difficulties that make one all the more determined to go.

During our conversations in the summer of 1960, we had discussed the fact that his books were coming back into print, not only in Russia but also in English-speaking countries. Many of his expert translations were reappearing in America. He said that his version of *Candide* had long been pirated there. Remembering an unforgettable phrase from an anonymous translation I had used in teaching college courses, I asked if it were his: Cunégonde had "been raped to the limit of possibility." Richard smiled, and nodded: ". . . après avoir été violée autant qu'on peut l'être."

I suggested that some of the paperback editors there

might be interested in reissuing *Death of a Hero* and some of the other novels. Richard felt—rightly as it turned out—that publishers wouldn't take to the idea; in the American mood of that time, *Hero* was particularly unsuitable. It had been reprinted as a paperback in England, however, in 1958, and Richard told me (21 December 1961), "The other day I worked out that in England alone the Hero has sold at least 130,000. It never caught on in U.S.A.—too British I expect—but it has been translated into at least 10 languages." Not long before (8 December 1961) he had told me, "There has been such a run on the paperback of my Lawrence of Arabia that it had passed 42,000 in June (my last figure) and had run so high that the publishers were caught napping, sold out, and are waiting for the next reprint." In the same letter, he asked, "If the N.Y. Times Book Review use Dr. [Stanley] Weintraub's review of Nutting on TEL, will you clip it out and send? Weintraub is so far the only real scholar who has studied this 'queer' person and the evidence."

The Weintraub review arrived at a moment when I was writing a letter to Lawrence Durrell, so I sent him a copy and asked him to forward it, since he was in close touch with Richard, who wrote (1 January 1962):

Many thanks indeed for sending the Times cutting to Durrell. I am very glad to have a duplicate. Weintraub sent it to me, saying that the Times had "softened down" his criticism of Nutting by "judicious touches." Why? So far Weintraub is the only commentator on TEL I've read who knows the evidence first hand, and not just from the newspapers and propaganda of the Lawrence Bureau. When Cap Pearce [of Duell, Sloan and Pearce] was here in October, speaking as a publisher, he

said rather upstage that Americans aren't interested in TEL.
Phoeey. They're interested enough to make money out of the
myth, via Sam Spiegel [the film producer] and even Nutting.
Why not give honest American readers a chance to look at the
other side?

In discussing T. E. Lawrence with Richard, I always
found him healthily cynical on the subject, never vitriolic
or enraged. Alister Kershaw had requested him to write
the biography, a task he had undertaken with reluctance.
He didn't know where it was going to lead, though it can
hardly be denied that he was pleased when he made some
Establishment-shaking discoveries.

As we sat there on the day of my last visit to Sury,
Richard spoke of Hart Crane, whom he used to see drunk
at the Paris sidewalk cafés and of Thomas Wolfe, whose
enthusiastic and extravagant gestures Richard amusingly
imitated. One of his funniest stories was about T. S. Eliot,
who through Richard's influence was taken onto the *Times
Literary Supplement* as a leader writer in the early 1920's.
Richard arranged for Eliot to meet the *TLS* editor, Bruce
Richmond, at lunch in Soho. Eliot, just back from Switzerland, appeared wearing an Uncle Sam chin whisker, looking like an American stage-version of a hillbilly. Richmond
looked startled, but was soon under the spell of Eliot's talk,
and engaged him for the *Times*.

As Richard spoke of those days, the scenes beyond his
window were certainly right out of Pol de Limborg's *Très
Riches Heures*. Richard told an amusing story of a local
winegrower who resented the tax imposed on every bottle
moved from a vigneron's cellars to his own bistro across

the town. This winegrower and his friends dug a tunnel
under the town, from the cellar to the bistro and store,
and so the proprietor evaded the tax.

As we went from Maison Sallé out into the country
again, I discovered a little-known aspect of Richard: he
was an expert on butterflies. I evidently remarked on that
in a subsequent letter, for he wrote me about this interest
the following spring from Saintes-Maries, Bouches-du-
Rhône (29 March 1961), using a word that seems to come
naturally to some of the elder British intellectuals, though
it is one which American liberals avoid:

In USA the Clouded Yellow butterfly become more and more
orange as you go South or West. It's the same here. In Sury
they are sulphur-yellow, and here part or wholly orange. One of
my griefs is the destruction of my personal collection of American Lepidoptera—made on a Florida sandbarren, the Lawrence
Ranch, and the desert round L.A. They were packed and sent
to Jamaica, where I hoped to add to them. But they arrived
while there was some political struggle with the niggers, who
intentionally threw down the crates they were landing from
ships. Nine-tenths of the collection, the work of nearly seven
years, was smashed to bits—I just gave up. One can't fight barbarians in that force. Those cases were strong, good, US packing,
and simply smashed by ill usage. There were some interesting
varieties of butterfly up on the ranch, but I had some really rare
specimens from the Mohave. I had also some specimens of a
Fritillary bred from caterpillars taken off a passion-fruit vine on
Sunset Boulevard!

Another topic we discussed was one of Richard's last
books, *Introduction to Mistral,* for whose American edition I had had the honor of writing a preface. The volume

had originally been published by Heinemann in London in 1956; a few years later the director of the Southern Illinois University Press, Vernon Sternberg, became interested in the book, but Richard had little hope for it in the United States, even after it had won an important prize in 1959. He wrote (13 April 1959):

I sent off last week the announcement of the award of the Prix de Gratitude Mistralienne. It pleases me, but of course the Anglo-Americans know nothing about Mistral, and proved unwilling to learn when I published the book. America wouldn't publish it, and England didn't read it. One happy result is that it has made Catherine persona grata in the Midi, and she went to a ferrade (i.e. cattle-branding) by invitation yesterday. I still don't know what the dough is—probably 100,000 francs, no great shakes but better than a kick in the pants.

His predictions about the Mistral book were too dire. The English edition sold out completely, and the American volume was also a success, heralded in the spring of 1960 by Henri Peyre's friendly and perceptive review in *The New York Times*. For a series, Crosscurrents/Modern Critiques, which I began editing for Southern Illinois University Press, I suggested that Richard write a small book on the Imagists, but his doctors had forbidden him to undertake any more full-length volumes. He was under contract to Encyclopaedia Britannica, Inc., for a volume on world poetry, and this, with all his correspondence, was his principal literary activity in his last years. He asked for suggestions, both as to recent American poets and good translations by Americans; he wrote (28 September 1959) that the former would be ruled out by a decision "to stick to the original limit; No Living Poets. This is a great pity, but either I shall have to wreck the whole structure to get them in, or the book will be unwieldy." Roy Campbell's widow had sent him some translations by Campbell, who had been one of his best friends: "In the preface to Roy's book Edith Sitwell says his translation of Juan de la Crux's Noche Sombre is one of the greatest poems of our times. . . . I just don't see it. It seems to me one of his rare failures, and I'm keeping the version I already had by an unknown girl named Ida Farnell. His Lorca are first-rate."

Writing again about his editorial problems (12 October 1959), he said in part:

I wish I could have had a few more translations by living poets (most of my translators are scholars!) but they are damned unenterprising, always the same Baudelaire, Rilke, Verlaine, Rimbaud, Lorca, Valéry—I am up to my neck in them! They are all so anxious to be "dong le mouvemong" (as Ezra used to say very seriously) that they daren't explore literature outside the fashionable fence-rails. I want a good translation of one or two of those poems Fortunatus Venentius wrote to St Radegund, and I want ONE decent translation of Carducci, and of Boethius. I believe I'll have to use Chaucer's version of Boethius, ridiculous as it sounds, but the Loeb isn't much good. . . .

One of his literary efforts in those last years was his defense of *Lady Chatterley's Lover* against an American woman author; his letter (7 December 1959) refers to her and to two Lawrence books I had edited:

Katherine Anne Porter has written an article on *Lady C.* of the usual "anti" kind, reiterating the old arguments, for *En-*

counter. They ask me to reply. I've got so much on hand about DHL at the moment that I would have refused, but it must be done at once and you are up to your neck in Lawrentiana. Luckily the Sex and Censorship book arrived Sat. and the Miscellany today. I have asked [Melvin J.] Lasky to let me peg the article on them, replying to Porter briefly. Of course, that crowd is still so anti-Lawrence they think KAP's custard is terrific.

As much as Richard liked Lawrence's work, *Lady Chatterley's Lover* wasn't one of his enthusiasms. When I told him I had reviewed the Grove Press break-through edition for *The New York Times,* he wrote (13 April 1959):

I don't envy you the job of reviewing the unexpurgated Lady C. The thought is perhaps unworthy, but from the beginning I have wondered if DHL were not a little hopeful to cash in on the pornographic market of Ulysses, especially as his royalties were declining rapidly. I think the book is one of his least good novels, in spite of brilliant passages. No doubt the "words" are basic Saxon and were used innocently in the Middle Ages, but they have unluckily been incrusted with nastiness, and they cannot in this age be used with the purity DHL claimed. The author is not a dictator of language—he must take into account the use of it by the people.

Richard had nevertheless, in 1928, helped distribute the copies of the book which were smuggled into England. He relates, in *Life for Life's Sake,* how Lawrence wrote him "a long letter in which he urged me to tell everybody what a great book it was, 'a feather in the cap of the twentieth century'; and naturally I neither did nor should use such a silly phrase. Judge of my delight when I read his *Letters* and found he had written round to other people: 'Richard Aldington says *Lady C.* is a feather in the cap of the twentieth century.' "

It was one thing, however, for Richard to jest at Lawrence's expense; he defended him from others. He told me (13 December 1959) that he was sending me a carbon copy of his *Encounter* articles: "Do you think my salute of '21 mews' to KAP is caddish? Perhaps I'd better tell Lasky to cut it." Further:

I wanted to take up the topic of the resentment of the rentier intellectuals at Lawrence's atrocious behaviour at making fun of them in Women in Love and Aaron's Rod. But there wasn't room. What harm did it do them? Only a few people at the time knew who was meant. What could be more fatuous than keeping up the resentment 20 years after his death, as Norman Douglas and [Cecil] Gray did—getting together in a London club (with a war on!) and talking about being "stabbed in the back." L's caricatures of N. D. did Douglas no harm whatever, but Douglas's Magnus pamphlet was spiteful and vindictive, and did harm Lawrence. The thing is damnably "weasel-worded" and tries cunningly to insinuate that DHL was responsible for Magnus's suicide, when DHL paid his hotel bill and gave him money, while his beloved friend Douglas didn't give him a cent.

Richard himself was in *Aaron's Rod,* with a bit part: Robert Cunningham, who "drank red wine in large throatfuls." I've also wondered whether Richard weren't also, at least in part, the officer named Herbertson who chatters about the war; surely this is to some extent the younger Herbert Asquith who, like Richard, talked with Lawrence during leaves from the battlefront.

99

"Stabbed in the back" or not, Richard proved a loyal supporter of Lawrence, as his several books and pamphlets on him show; as we have seen, he was even willing to rally to the defense of *Lady Chatterley's Lover,* a novel about which he was hardly enthusiastic. Certainly Richard, who saw Lawrence without illusion but was sympathetic to him and his work, did him a great deal of good with his support over the years—more so, for example, than some who were operating a kind of Lawrence-for-God club. And he could see the comic aspects of Lawrence, as shown in a letter (22 November 1961) from Aix, enclosing an English newspaper article headed: "Husband Broke Saucer Over Wife's Head." The article prompted Richard to comment, "You'll see at once that this Lancelot du Lac of low life has combined in one effective scene two of the more discreditable incidents in the love life of Lorenzo and Frieda. Is it unconscious plagiarism, or had he read our books?"

If Richard was knocked about a bit in *Aaron's Rod,* H. D. came off somewhat better, as Julia, "a tall stag of a thing" who "sat hunched up like a witch. Yet she had real beauty." Lawrence also introduced Cecil Gray, whose love affair with H. D. is reflected in her own novel, *Bid Me To Live.* Lawrence shows her "talking to the young man, who was not her husband: a fair, pale, fattish fellow in pince-nez and dark clothes. This was Cyril Scott, a friend," who in *Bid Me To Live* was called Vane.

Lawrence in his letters explored the H. D.-Cecil Gray relationship rather fully. Richard's comments (23 October 1959) on my information about this have already been quoted. He replied more vigorously later. This came about in the following way.

Both David Garnett and Richard, who were not friendly to one another, kindly offered, in 1960, to go over the proofs of Lawrence's *Collected Letters* for me—a kindness of the sort that is never possible to repay. Their help, particularly about aspects of British Life and numerous men and women Lawrence referred to in his correspondence, was invaluable. And both of them were good sports in the matter of Lawrence's nasty remarks about them in the letters. I have already quoted Richard on the subject; because David Garnett was equally above the battle, the number of blank spaces or asterisks of omission could be reduced. But, as always, Richard was sensitive on the score of H. D. Two paragraphs which dealt with matters H. D. herself had made use of in *Bid Me To Live* were particularly dangerous, Richard felt (5 June 1961):

The criminal libel situation must be cleared up. As I told you, H. D. is sick in Zürich, under doctor's orders to have complete rest for a few days. I didn't like to write direct for fear of upsetting her. But I heard an old friend was visiting, communicated with her, and asked if she could tactfully find out if Hilda has in fact seen the two paragraphs and given permission. A cable just in with answer: "indignant No." So you will either have to get clearance from her and Dorothy Yorke—sending them the exact text—or risk a prosecution and injunction for libel in both countries. Do attend to this at once, Harry. We can't afford to risk this. Alister is here, and he thinks most unquestionably that the two paras are libellous.

The two offending "paras," which occurred in different parts of the *Collected Letters,* were of course excised.

A few months after the letter from Richard quoted above, H. D. died. Richard wrote about this from Aix (14 October 1961).

Catha arrived [at Sury], and we drove to Zürich, where H. D.'s friend put us up at the very comfortable Hotel Glockenhof—which has Bibles in the bedrooms, the first time I ever saw that outside the US. At the last minute the two specialists only allowed C. to visit H. D.—I suspect she didn't want her former husband to see her in that state. Catha reported "Hilda looks very sick." There was nothing we could do, so we returned (by car) to Sury, to pick up books etc; and then rather rushed to the Saintes where C. was booked to take part in some local fête with bulls and horses. . . . On the morning of the 27th Sept. H. D. received and looked over an advance copy of her "Helen" poem, sent by Pearson, and was pleased and interested. She died that night, and was cremated on the 2nd Oct. (anniversary of her wedding!) in Zürich. The ashes will be flown home, and will be placed beside her parents in Bethlehem, Pa. She had been just fifty years in Europe.

Richard felt that the obituaries in both America and England, although fairly accurate, gave too little indication of H. D.'s genius. *The Times* (London), however, printed "some notes from Herbert Read, very sensitive and perceptive indeed, though he does not realise how much of the experience in the early poems was not 'Greek' but came from Maine and Penna., though of course she used Greek symbols."

So far, only snippets from Richard Aldington's letters have been quoted. Here is an entire letter, written at the beginning of what was to prove to be the last year of his life, a letter wonderfully characteristic of the man, his humor, and his lively interest in people and events:

Hotel de Sévigné
Aix-en-Provence
B. du R.
18/1/62

Dear Harry,

Durrell came over at lunchtime yesterday, and went off again this morning. I expected him to be a little frayed, since he is stuck in the third act of a new play, but he was his usual serene self, still with a trace of Foreign Office urbanity. Still, he must be pre-occupied since he admitted that he made three false starts—had to go back and pick up things he'd forgotten, one of which was his chequebook! Here he discovered that he had also forgotten to bring his car papers—rather serious if the police happened to ask for them. So he rang up Claude [Mrs. Durrell], and to his vexation couldn't get through. On the third try he had an altercation with the Nîmes phone girl, and then found that just after he left the PTT had changed his old telephone for a dial, and of course had changed the number. He arranged for the papers to be sent express to the British Consul in Marseille, and decided to risk the drive there to pick them up. Hope all goes well.

He says that Miller is out of financial trouble (temporarily) having sold the movie rights of a book for $65,000. There is always a suspicion of oriental arithmetic in Larry's figures, so we'd better not take that too literally. I only hope H.M. may have something left after taxes and [James] Laughlin. Gerald Durrell has sold My Family & Other Animals (for an unspecified large sum) to be adapted as a Broadway farce and movie. Shooting of the Alexandria quartet (which Fox have paid for) is held up until this interminable Cleopatra is out of the way, and they decide whether or no Liz Taylor is to be Justine.

If Larry escapes the police and gets his papers he is going to see a friend near Grasse, and will drop in here again on his way home. He is always most interested in asking questions about the writers he never knew and I at least met or knew well, such as Conrad, Yeats, Hueffer, DHL, Brooke, Maugham, De la Mare, etc. He is very anti-Ezra, and says he has tangled with Eliot over that.

A very pleasant visit, though rather tiring for me—and I had to eat two meals instead of my usual one.

A point in DHL's letters came up. You may remember L. wrote somebody I was returning to the front, and I had said "As for me I go unto my Father" which he thought "a bit thick." Of course I wasn't comparing myself to Christ, and either intentionally or unintentionally L. mistook a joke. Before going back to the trenches, the British tommies were regaled with a short C. of E. service, which almost always began with the text: "I will arise and go unto my Father, and say 'Father I have sinned etc.'" This struck the troops as not very appropriate to the job ahead of them, and they parodied it: "I will arise and go unto my Father, and say 'STANDING, LOAD.'" (A British musketry order.) I can't swear it, but I must have told this to L. since he was disdainfully interested in the trench "life." Intentionally or unintentionally he took my joke literally, though I never set up as a Saviour of the World, and duly passed his censure. Amusingly characteristic.

I haven't seen the book, but there is one out by Lina Waterfield "Castle in Italy." You remember that in early 1914 in Lerici, the L.s were visited by three Georgian poets and "a man named Waterfield"—Aubrey Waterfield. It was the usual thing —friendship and then rows. If the book comes out in USA, you'll probably get it for review. Mrs. Waterfield was correspondent in Italy for the London Observer.

Catha has exchanged her intractable horse for a much younger one, which (she says) should be much easier to break in.

After watching for a couple of hours the vicious kicking, rearing and bucking, not to mention rolling, that goes on, I decided I wouldn't care for horse-breaking as a job.

Hope all is well with you,

All the best,

Richard.

In the summer of 1962, Richard and his daughter went to Russia. They were guests of the Writers' Union, whose secretary, Alexei Surkov, the opponent of Boris Pasternak, had written to Richard in February that the organization wanted to honor a writer whose books were so widely read and loved in Soviet Russia; the Writers' Union would pay all travel expenses for Richard and his daughter between Paris and Moscow, and would entertain them for three weeks, celebrating Richard's seventieth birthday.

He went, and the strain must have been too great; he died soon after getting back, a day or so after writing me a last letter telling how pleasant it had all been.

To write these reminiscences of Richard Aldington so soon after his death has been in many ways a saddening experience: it evokes times lost. His letters to me, only a small part of which are quoted from, represent an eager and generous giving-forth of life; they are so incandescently alive to me that on rereading them I find myself constructing answers which, alas, can not be sent. But the melancholy of the occasion is relieved by gladness, for the memories and the letters are of the kind that make life good. It is good, too, to know that Richard Aldington went out on a high moment, like the Voltaire he so much admired, amid fêtes and praises.

Lawrence Clark Powell

Soon after I became Librarian of UCLA on July 1, 1944, I found a letter to my predecessor from Archibald Macleish, the Librarian of Congress, introducing Richard Aldington, newly come to Los Angeles and desirous of library privileges. I wrote at once to Aldington, offering my personal services, in addition to whatever the library was already doing for him, remarking on our mutual friendship with Frieda Lawrence and my own long standing admiration for him as a novelist, poet, critic, and translator.

A few days later my secretary announced Mr. Aldington and in came a big, handsome, jovial man, accompanied by Netta, his lovely Scottish wife, and their six-year-old daughter Catherine, snub-nosed, freckle-faced, gap-toothed, and mischievous.

We hit it off and for the next two years an increasingly warm friendship developed between Richard and me, my wife Fay and Netta, and our two boys, Norman and

Wilkie and Catha. Books and butterflies were our bonds, as well as food and France.

Aldington was both bookman and entomologist. His letters are equally full of book talk to me and butterfly talk to Norman.

Why doesn't your university press issue a complete illustrated moths of America, and a corpus of Elizabethan drama complete? I want both these works. Tell Norman that on Sunday one of the Swallowtails emerged from the pupa. He was a lovely specimen with more blue on the wings than in any Asterius I have seen. Unscientific sentimentalism has kept it out of my collection. I felt I couldn't kill so lovely a creature on the very verge, so to speak, of the cradle. So I let it go. Perhaps one day Norman will collect some of its descendants.

Aldington had come to Los Angeles to write Hollywood scripts. We never discussed this aspect of his writing and the only reference to it in the many letters he wrote me (although his home in an apartment building next to Ciro's Restaurant on the Sunset Strip was only a couple of miles from campus) reads,

Not half an hour after you left came a telephone call. Miss —————— ————— has changed, what is laughingly referred to as her "mind," and doesn't want the script after all, and so I don't have to rewrite it.

What was he writing? A variety of things, and with great vigor and competence. A novel based on Casanova's memoirs. A book about the English aesthetes of the eighteen-nineties, for which he was scouring the local bookshops for their works, as well as drawing on the UCLA Library for reference books. An anthology of Oscar Wilde for the Viking Portable series to which the University's William Andrews Clark Memorial Library contributed twelve unpublished Wilde letters. Aldington's introduction to this volume is one of the best things ever written about Wilde.

We visited back and forth at their Sunset apartment, where once Norman and Wilkie commandeered the elevator and took Catha up and down a hundred times, until the manager restored order; and in our homes in Beverly Glen and Westwood. Netta painted Fay's portrait in half a dozen versions. Richard instructed our wives how to make an omelette à la mode française and the boys how to care for a butterfly collection. His letters to me are crammed with book talk and blasts at the bureaucrats of all countries.

In April of 1946 the Aldingtons left Los Angeles, driving via Arizona and Texas to New Orleans and thence by plane to Miami and Kingston, Jamaica, from where Richard sent me a bottle of genuine bay rum which had been unavailable during the war.

By the end of the year he wrote me from Paris:

I heard from Al Manuel (his agent) that all the Christmas trees and Santas were out on Hollywood Boulevard again, and that nearly every street had its own real Christmas tree. Well, I can imagine it all, and the overcrowded car-parks, the crowd buying turkeys at the Farmer's Market, and those lovely Santa Monica hills, and the sun and the palms, and I could almost cry for homesickness. Just buy Catherine a ten-cent ice-cream cone, will you, and eat it all to yourself on the library stairway.

Thenceforth we were in steady correspondence. Fay and I spent 1950/51 in Europe on sabbatical and we planned to be with Richard and his daughter for Christmas at Le Lavandou in the south of France, but cold weather prevented us from keeping the rendezvous. That, and our friendship with Netta in London, possibly annoyed Richard and eight years passed before he wrote again.

I heard from him last the month before he died, telling me of the trip to Moscow for his seventieth birthday celebration and hailing our planned reunion at Sury-en-Vaux in the spring of 1963. Alas, he was gone before we reached France.

Sir Alec Randall

I don't think that those writers—English writers, at any rate—who wrote about Richard Aldington after his lamented death can possibly have known him personally. Otherwise they would surely have emphasised his generous nature, his kindliness, his sense of humour, his deep affection, love of children and essentially tolerant, scholarly and civilised outlook which, to those who knew him well, shone through all his disillusionment and frustration. The writers I have mentioned based themselves on one or two of his books, a long list of poems, novels, biographies and criticism, and spoke of him as an "angry young man," as constantly frustrated and embittered, as a deliberate denigrator of writers he disapproved of. Now, even his closest friends would admit that there was an element of truth in this. His novel, *Death of a Hero* (1929), which made him famous, was certainly the work of an "angry young man." His experience of the First World War had excited his indignation against the men who had, he thought, in

their blindness and folly, sent the flower of a whole generation to their death, or to appalling suffering endured
on the Somme or in the mud of Flanders. He described
all this with a realism and sincerity which evoked, for
example, the admiration of H. G. Wells and continued to
sell his book at home and abroad till the end of his life.
Like Remarque's *Im Westen nichts Neues,* it is a classic
of the war of 1914 to 1918. Not having myself suffered
the things he saw and endured in active service, I am not
in a position to discuss them or Richard's reaction to them.
But I can say that his anger seems to me to have had a far
greater dignity and sense of human values than the cynical
and tedious work of certain "angry young men" after the
Second World War. I will be frank and admit also that
Richard did feel that he had been unjustifiably neglected.
He often spoke impetuously with contempt of England
and the United States, and declared that he would never
set foot in them again. This was not taken well by generous friends, admiring friends whom he had in both
countries. His final offence was that he exploded the "heroic legend" of T. E. Lawrence; this also caused annoy-
ance in both countries. He insisted, in one of the last
talks I had with him, that he had not—unlike Lytton
Strachey—started out with the intention of "debunking"
his subject. The work was commissioned and he made it
his primary task to consult all the written sources, gather
all the personal testimonies, study every word Lawrence
wrote and check it against other narratives. It all required
immense, painstaking industry and, whatever we may
think of the result, with its undeniable bias, no one can
overlook the essential value of Richard's researches to future

biographers of Lawrence. The attacks on the book irritated him intensely and he set to work to gather material to substantiate his criticisms, which was used in the revised edition. His friends regretted this obsession. In New York friends of his begged me to persuade him to divert his talents and energies into another novel. They prophesied— his American literary agent told me—that another novel like *All Men are Enemies* (1933) would be a best seller. I wrote accordingly to Richard, but he said he felt he didn't have another novel in him. I then asked him to consider another suggestion, namely a history of English literature just before the First World War, the poets and novelists of Harold Monro's Poetry Bookshop, the American immigration, Ezra Pound, John Gould Fletcher, T. S. Eliot, Amy Lowell and Richard's wife Hilda Doolittle, the blossoming of the Imagist School until it was killed by the war. But Richard refused, and in a letter to me some months before his death he told me he felt he could write no more.

But I must return to my original intention, which is to speak of Richard as I knew him. We first met when he was about nineteen, as undergraduates at University College, University of London. There Richard became the centre of a group of admiring friends, of whom I was one —though not the closest. Closer to Richard then was a young man called Arthur Chapman, and I was closer to him than I was to Richard. Both Richard and Arthur wrote poetry but Richard, with his handsome features, his sparkling merry eyes, his reddish beard and velvet jacket and flowing bow tie was the more romantic figure.

He was also a rebel. His presence at University College

was due to his refusal to conform to his mother's ambition
and enter a regular profession. She was a writer, author of
a successful but now forgotten book called *Love-letters
that never reached him*. Richard despised this; he also
wanted to be a writer, but not that kind. He had tried
journalism but had given it up when he found he was
assigned to the reporting of local football matches. His
defiance of authority, which was gay and far from angry,
his enthusiasm for modern French poetry—all this delighted us, and communicated itself to us. Then one day,
in the summer of 1911, during the vacation, came the
news that Arthur Chapman had been drowned. It was
a grievous loss to our circle of friends. Arthur's father
brought out a volume of his poems and other writings,
and included letters to him from Richard. All very youthful, the poems much influenced by Rossetti, the young
Yeats or the French Symbolists. My friendship with
Arthur and then the friendship I continued with Richard
widened my outlook. I was studying English literature
under W. P. Ker, Latin under A. E. Housman, French
under Louis Brandin and German under Hans Priebsch.
I came from a nonconformist home, puritanical but not
severe or excessively prudish; but my parents' world was
very narrow and they had their particular antipathies; they
disliked Roman Catholicism, which they vaguely hinted
was immoral; they were firmly opposed to all alcoholic
drinks, and they thought that theatregoing, except school
performances of Shakespeare and entertainments like the
Negro minstrels, were not only a waste of money, but a
step on the way to moral ruin. Until I was grown up I
do not think my parents had ever been to a professional

theatre, and it was not only early poverty that held them back.

To Richard and his circle this was quite incomprehensible, and before long I was going with Richard and the others to dinner in a Soho French restaurant, where, I remember, we got a table d'hôte dinner for a shilling and a bottle of very drinkable wine for two shillings; we also went to the theatre and opera when we could afford it. Most of us were wholehearted Wagnerians and Shavians; politically we were Fabian Socialists and champions of votes for women. On this Richard stood rather apart from us. He was inclined to be anti-German—though he had once, he told me, met on the train between Rome and Paris the German poet Stefan George, who delighted him. In any case Richard did not join in the anti-Verdi or even the anti-Puccini clique to which the Wagner-enthusiasts belonged. We were all, I think, converted from it in later years, but Richard's first love was always France, and then Italy, their literature, their music and their people. As for politics Richard was a thorough individualist, and remained so all his life. He preferred the "pure art" of Wilde and Yeats to Shaw's political social tracts dressed up as drama. He could not share our enthusiasm for the social reform ideas of Mr. and Mrs. Sidney Webb, those dessicated but influential Socialist economists, with whom Wells quarrelled, and who were to live to eulogise the social and political system they found established in Moscow. Richard was by no means a snob, but there was about him then a trace of the Horatian "odi profanum vulgus et arceo." As he grew older the manipulation of the masses by politicians through a highly centralised government became

more and more antipathetic to him. He was, I think, no-
where so happy as in his beloved Provence, next door to
which he lived, in Montpellier, so many years; Provence,
by whom he was honoured, and to whom he gave his
biography of Mistral. Even in Provence, however, the
heavy hand of a strong central government could be felt,
and once he told me that the people of Avignon regretted
they were not under the absolute but mild and unexacting
rule of the Papacy; and he agreed with them.

At University College the professors I have named
were distinguished scholars and stimulating teachers. The
academic curriculum, however, imposed limitations on
them. Housman, for example, taught us, in his drily
humorous, severe fashion, to appreciate Virgil, Livy,
Cicero and above all Tacitus. Richard, for his part, was
scornful of "old chick-pea" (Cicero) and advised me to
drop him and read Catullus. He introduced me to the
mediaeval Latin poets. At that time he was in correspondence with Remy de Gourmont, and gave me his *Le Latin
Mystique,* which opened up for me a new, wonderful
world. I have sometimes thought that this was one of the
influences which led me, a few years later, to become a
Catholic. It certainly encouraged me to study the lovely
Latin hymns, and led me on to the writings of St. Augus-
tine. Richard used to tease me about my conversion, but
always kindly and gently. He would also try shocking me,
as when one day he sent me from the Western Front a
postcard photograph of him and his fellow-officers inscribed simply "Ecce homo, inter latrones." When I was
appointed to be secretary at the British Legation to the
Holy See he gave me a copy of the *Index Librorum pro-*

hibitorum, which was accompanied by a note saying "This will cramp your style, my boy!" Incidentally Richard's father became a Catholic late in life and Richard inherited his library. He showed it to me one day when he was living in a cottage in Berkshire, on the banks of the River Kennet; it contained many classics of Christian literature.

As with Latin, so with English and French literature; Richard always wanted to go beyond the academic horizon. He was in touch with writers of the time, English and French. Later, from outside the circle at University College, came F. S. Flint, an omniscient authority on current French poetry. Frank also published poems of his own and his theory of "cadence" had a part in the development of the Imagist school. Richard introduced me to Harold Monro, of the Poetry Bookshop, which gained a great reputation as a place where modern poetry was studied and read aloud. Both there and in Yeats's room over a shop off the Euston Road—a rather squalid part of London then— I heard W. B. Yeats speaking his own poetry. This unforgettable experience I also owed to Richard.

My friendship with Richard continued when, in 1913, I went off to the University of Tübingen. Richard had become the editor of a curious little review, the *Egoist,* which, I always understood, was financed by Dora Marsden, so as to give her a place in which to expound her complex and, to me at any rate, incomprehensible philosophy. The importance of the *Egoist* was that it gave Richard and his friends the basis they needed on which to build up the Imagist school of poetry. One of the best of the Imagist poets was Hilda Doolittle, an American who wrote under the initials "H. D.," and appears so in several anthologies of English or American poetry. Perhaps she was the best of them, the inspirer. Richard married her and wrote some of his best poems under her influence. At first they lived in Mecklenburgh Square, in Bloomsbury, but they had nothing to do with what came to be called the "Bloomsbury Set," Virginia Woolf, Roger Fry, Clive Bell, John Maynard Keynes and Lytton Strachey. The Mecklenburgh Square group included, at one time or another, D. H. Lawrence, John Cournos, the American Russian writer, Arundel del Ré, a critic and poet of Italian origin, Amy Lowell, John Gould Fletcher, both American poets. When I returned from Germany in August, 1914, escaping into Belgium before the German invasion, I went to live at Mecklenburgh Square, and saw the first Zeppelin over London dropping bombs about five hundred yards from where John Cournos and I were standing. Richard and H. D. took a flat in Hampstead, and when I married about eighteen months later my wife and I took a flat in the same block.

We were all poor then but, struggling writer though Richard was, he always showed a generous sympathy to those who were suffering from the same disadvantages. Where he could not give direct help, he tried to find them remunerative literary work. Some of those he helped, either then or in later years, rose to eminence in the literary world. Richard had been working for Ford Madox Hueffer, the novelist, and finding that he wanted an assistant with a knowledge of German and the Germans, suggested me. Ford engaged me to help him in writing two propaganda books, *When Blood is their Argument* and *Between St. Denis and St. George,* with which the

British Government designed to counteract Bernard Shaw's writings against the war. In this way, Richard not only made me acquainted with that exasperating but endearing figure, Ford Madox Ford (as he later named himself), whose great merits as a novelist have only recently received proper recognition, but he also, indirectly, put me in touch with the British official world. This was, eventually, after the end of the war, to bring me into the diplomatic service, where I spent most of my life.

While Richard was away at the war his marriage with H. D. broke up. It was, in all its circumstances, a shattering experience for Richard, and I have often thought that it, with his war-experiences, did much to inspire the bitterness he was later to express. It must be said, however, that the estrangement from H. D. was not permanent. One day, in the fifties, when Richard was living in Montpellier and H. D. somewhere near Zurich, he wrote asking me whether I could help her with her passport and American visa. With tenderness he reminded me that H. D. was not very practical, and was confronted with the problem of obtaining an American visa on her British passport, which she had kept as a British subject by marriage long after her divorce from Richard. She succeeded in getting back to the United States and, as Richard rather proudly informed me, had a great success with her lectures and with her book about her friendship with Sigmund Freud. A year or so later Richard, at the end of one of his letters, said that H. D. sent her love with his to my wife and me. I replied asking him to give H. D. our most affectionate greetings, and received in return a letter from Richard telling me that it was too late; H. D. had died. Richard's grief and his pride in her fame were touching to observe.

Between the two world wars I was out of England for most of the time, but Richard and I continued to correspond. He came to see us in Rome a number of times between 1926 and 1930, and instantly became very popular with my small children. Then I went down with typhoid and was very seriously ill for some months. Richard wrote consolingly to my wife, and later told me that at one time the news was so desperate that he had written my obituary. There wasn't much to record, and he never showed it to me. At length I was convalescent and was, with my wife, installed in a hotel at Vallombrosa. Our children had been sent to England with their Italian nurse to stay with my wife's parents. My wife felt she must go and bring them back to Italy, but was anxious about leaving me alone. One day she said "I know what I will do; I'll ask Richard." She telegraphed and received an immediate reply. Within a day or two Richard arrived, accompanied by Dorothy Yorke. It was a characteristic generous response, and I know I am not by any means the only friend of his who has received such kindness. He was the ideal companion for a convalescent, so thoughtful and adaptable, so gay and cheerful. He was then doing his translation of the *Decameron,* and I remember his discussing various words with me. His version became the standard one in English. When I was completely recovered and back at work in Rome he came to see us, enlivening us all with his talk and delighting the children with his fun. But it was not long before I was moved to Bucharest, and we lost touch. We resumed our correspondence after the Second World War, and in 1953, when I was sent as one of the

United Kingdom delegates to the United Nations—it was my first visit to New York—he gave me several introductions to friends of his and so created precious new friendships for me. I did not see him again until the summer of 1956 when, after official business in Geneva, I went on to stay with him at Montpellier. There I met his delightful daughter, so much loved by him. He seemed to be his old self, full of humour and kindliness; for lunch that day of reunion I noted he ordered a bottle of Château Mouton-Rothschild of first-class vintage. It was a happy occasion, but for me it was overshadowed by the fact that Richard seemed to be living in very straitened circumstances; his combined bedroom, sitting room and library was in such confusion that I wondered how he could possibly work there. The second disturbing fact was Richard's obsession with the feud his book on T. E. Lawrence had stirred up. On most days Catha drove Richard and me round Provence, and we were very gay. But one afternoon he asked me to stay with him and go over the large correspondence which his biography had provoked. He eagerly showed me letters from contemporaries or fellow-officers of Lawrence which corroborated his interpretation of the facts. These, as I have mentioned, were used in the revised edition. To me it seemed a pity that Richard was so much bogged down in such a sterile controversy. Later, I thought I had annoyed him by writing him a full account of Terence Rattigan's play *Ross,* which, I told him, seemed to me to present a balanced view of an enigmatic character. There were some weeks of silence, and then Richard wrote one of his usual friendly letters, with some banter about my having come under the spell of "the Prince of Mecca."

Richard thought long and anxiously before deciding to accept an invitation to visit the Soviet Union. His books, and especially his *Death of a Hero,* had a large sale in the Soviet Union, and royalties in roubles had accumulated there. When he asked me for an opinion I said that if he went at the invitation of Soviet writers, made no political speeches, and was careful, in the inevitable press-interviews, to say nothing that could be used as Communist propaganda, then I thought he should go. At length he decided to do so, accompanied by Catha. He did not write to me after his return; death suddenly cut him off. But I understand that he was very well received by the Soviet Russian writers, and enjoyed an interesting trip. It helped him to overcome his sense of frustration, his feeling that, in spite of large sales for two or three of his books, his first-class *Anthology of the Poetry of the English-speaking peoples,* and some of his translations, he was not appreciated. On the whole, it seems to me, Richard had not had a happy life; he was so often beset by personal problems and anxieties, and it is no mitigation to say they were sometimes brought upon him by himself. Ever since the end of the First World War he suffered from bouts of ill-health and in his later years he had bronchial trouble which would certainly have been made worse by living in England. He did not confide in me any of his domestic troubles, and the picture of Richard that will always be in my mind is that of a merry, humorous, kindly man. I think that it was this Richard, Richard in a time of happiness and contentment, who was so suddenly taken from the friends who loved him.

Sir Herbert Read

I first met Richard Aldington on some occasion when we were both on leave from the Front—I think it must have been late in 1916 or early 1917. I had for some years admired him as a poet and had eagerly read everything that he wrote for the *Egoist, Poetry and Drama,* and the *Little Review.* Groups of his poems had appeared in such anthologies as *Des Imagistes* (March, 1914), in *Some Imagist Poets* (1915) and *Some Imagist Poets 1916*—anthologies which he helped to edit. The prefactory manifestoes in these anthologies became my own poetic creed and Aldington's first volume of poems, *Images (1910–1915)*, which was published by The Poetry Bookshop (price 8d. net) with a coloured woodcut on its paper cover by John Nash, became one of my most treasured possessions—I still have it. I had looked forward to our meeting, therefore, with great eagerness and I was not disappointed. We immediately became friends and with intervals of silence due to war and exile, remained friends to the end. The last of many letters from him that have survived is dated 28/10/61—the first, written in pencil from his unit in France (inscribed "Ex vinculis") predates it by forty-two years.

I well remember that first meeting. We had lunch together and then strolled up Charing Cross Road, looking at the bookshops and talking about our literary enthusiasms. Aldington looked very handsome in his uniform and I was immediately captivated by the brightness and candour of his features—a boyishness, one might call it, which he retained perhaps all his life, certainly until he left Europe. He was one of the most stimulating friends I have ever had—easy in conversation and very frank, full of strange oaths (mostly in French), his mind darting about rapidly from one aspect of a subject to another. I was to spend many happy hours wtih him, at first in London and then, when he went to live at Malthouse Cottage, Padworth, on weekends which I spent there from time to time. It was a friendship not free from divergences of opinion—even fundamental differences of outlook, as I shall now try to explain.

After the war Aldington quickly re-established himself as an editor and reviewer. His main interest was French literature, of which he had a quite exceptional knowledge, but he was also a poet and with the publication of *Death of a Hero* in 1929, an outstanding novelist. But the progress from the imagist poet of 1915 to the novelist of 1929 was not accomplished without some strain on his own character and on our friendship. The first fact to realize is that sometime between the publication of the second Imagist anthology (1916) and the end of the war Aldington had abandoned his imagist ideals. We find Ezra Pound, in a letter to Margaret Anderson in August, 1917, already predicting that Imagism was finished as a movement. "I don't think any of these people have gone on; have invented much since the first *Des Imagistes* anthology." Pound had reasons of his own for dismissing the Imagists—there had been quarrels mainly due to the inclusion of Amy Lowell in the group—Pound detested her and her work. But there is more direct evidence of Aldington's own change of heart and style in a letter dated 29/3/22 which is in my possession though it was not written to me—I think the "mon cher" addressed in it must have been Harold Monro, and Monro must have passed it on to me since it gives a very careful and objective criticism of a collection of my own poems. They were subsequently published by the Hogarth Press (*Mutations of the Phoenix,* 1923), but I had perhaps first submitted them to the Poetry Bookshop. Aldington writes:

You will notice that the trend of the new school (as always) is to throw over its immediate predecessors. Thus our poetry was the poetry of the emotions and of beauty, of instinct and sudden impulse; it sought to share an "état d'âme"; its ideal of style was something clear, economical, exquisitely correct. Read (and others of his "school") try to create poetry from thought and the operations of the intelligence; psychology and character interest them; beauty is a phenomenon not a passion; they analyse love, they don't overflow with it. Instead of a jet of emotion immobilised by words into a silver fountain, they build a pillar of four dimensions cemented and rigid with intellect. Their style is allusive and elliptic; their vocabulary abstruse and ponderous; their meaning tenuous and remote. We limited our audience to those who feel intensely and delicately; they to those who think deeply and abundantly. We were sentimentalists; they are anatomists. We committed many follies, but they are wise; we were as silly as doves, but they as subtle as serpents. We secured a few hundred readers; they will have a few scores.

Aldington concluded (after further interesting comparisons): "I think he has done well in a genre I don't like. I commend him inasmuch as I am (or try to be) an impartial critic and I deplore him as a member of a rival sect." I myself would not have thought of myself as a member of a rival sect, but as the letter elsewhere makes clear, the rival sect that Aldington had in mind was that of T. S. Eliot. There is no doubt that Aldington from this time onwards became highly suspicious of, if not antagonistic towards, the direction that English writing was taking under the tutelage of Eliot. In answer to some friendly criticisms I had made of *A Fool i' the Forest,* the long poem Aldington published in 1924, he wrote:

If the Fool strikes you as a loose in structure, texture and idea, I reply that you call "loose" what I call ease, fluidity, clarity . . . Ten years, five years ago, I should have said Amen to your denunciation. Now, I take it as a compliment! I abandon, cast off, utterly deny the virtue of "extreme compression and essential significance of every word." I say that is the narrow path that leadeth to sterility. It makes a desert and you call it art. Pound, Flint, both went down on that; I saw them go; and I shall live to see you and Tom go the same way.

He then reveals his own new hopes:

I think this and the next decades of our lives should be a period of intense production and widening audience. God save

125

me from the fate of Pound and save you too! I say, pox on your intensities and essences; know what you know, feel what you feel, think what you think, and put it down, write, write, write!

The argument went on through several more letters, but they only served to make it clear that Aldington was now in full revolt against what he called the paradoxes and shibboleths of the intelligentsia. In a letter of 9/1/25 he writes:

I am rebelling against a poetry which I think too self-conscious, too intellectual, too elliptic and alembique. This poetry is (selon moi) distinguished by over-elaboration of thought and expression and by a costiveness of production.

And in the same letter there is this revealing passage:

I don't profess to know what Eliot's influence on me has been; I suspect that, like Pound's of old, it is rather negative than positive, warning me off, rather then luring me on. Like most English writers, I have found the one overwhelming influence to be Shakespeare. To escape it I fled to the French and to the Greeks, but to small avail. I find him in everything I write.

His letters become increasingly bitter in this year, but at the same time defiant. "I feel in a severely practical mood," he told me. "In answer to the question: For whom am I writing? As many people as will read me. Hence the necessity for as much energy and clarity and essential simplicity as one can compass." He began to write a series of articles for the newly established *Vogue,* and this led him to review "the whole movement from 1908 to the

126

present day." I do not know whether the planned series of sixteen articles was ever completed, or has survived, but it would have been of great historical interest. Here is a paragraph from an undated letter of this time that throws some welcome light on the origins of the Imagist movement:

I think it was a pity to drop that little sneer at the imagists but of course one must say what one honestly believes. I don't know what Pound got from Hulme, but I do know that my debt to Hulme = o. I disliked the man and still dislike him though he's dead. Also, I had written what Pound christened "imagist" poems before I had ever heard of Hulme. The point is that imagism, as written by H. D. and me, was purely our own invention and was not an attempt to put a theory in practice. The "school" was Ezra's invention. And the first imagist anthology was invented by him in order to claim us as his disciples, a manœuvre we were too naifs (*sic*) to recognise at the time, being still young enough to trust our friends.

There is another interesting confession in a letter of 2/7/25. He has been defending his use of the phrase "innate art sense" as an essential basis of criticism and writes:

By "innate art sense" I know I beg a dozen questions and probably write nonsense. But, as always, I here try to keep my eye on the fact. Now, between the ages of 15 and 16, the sight of Barfreston Church, a visit to the Musée Royale at Brussels, the discovery of English poetry, entirely changed my life. I recognised these things, without being told to do so, as a series of Columbus-like discoveries in my young life. My sister had exactly the same opportunities and remained entirely different. I conclude that I had an "innate art sense" and she hadn't.

A great deal of correspondence that follows towards the end of 1925 and through 1926 concerns a project called The Republic of Letters, a series of critical biographies he had undertaken to edit for Routledge. There was also to be a series of Broadway Translations, but the discussion of possible authors and impossible terms is perhaps not of general interest. There are some amusing letters about Voltaire, his own chosen author, and a refusal to discuss Dante (the Commedia "an imposing desert with marvellous oases, but these unfortunately become less frequent as the work proceeds"). He prefers Virgil.

In August, 1926, comes a sad and significant note: "I am very, very tired, more tired than I have ever been in my life and wondering if I am going to collapse. In fact, I feel damned ill." He went to Italy for a holiday and by the end of the year he was himself again, and accusing me of sounding a little weary—"overwork, my boy." "The mind doesn't get tired, but the nerves are something physical connected with thinking and writing do." He says in the same letter:

We saw a good deal of Lawrence in Italy—cantankerous and amusing as ever. He is hideously narrow-minded and too self-centred. But I like him very much, he is someone. He had a bug about founding an independent review, etc. I told him I thought independent reviews were bunk, and that for my part I can say all I have to say in reviews already established, that I see no point in writing for a few hundred people when you can say exactly the same thing to a good many thousands. So he revenged himself by saying I had no experience of the world.

For some time now Aldington's thought had been turning to the possibility of writing a novel with his war experience as a background. On 15/7/29 he writes:

I am sending you under another cover the proofs of 384 pages of my novel, and will forward the remainder as soon as they arrive. The proofs are for you alone—you know it's bad for a book to get about too much before publication. The English edition has been mutilated by the publishers, and I am trying to insist on the substitution of asterisks. In some places they have cut a whole page! God knows why, for it's pretty harmless. If you can spare time to read the novel, I'd like your comments, particularly on the war portions. At the point these proofs break off, there are still nearly 50 pages of war stuff to come. I hope you won't wholly disapprove—I always remember your saying that we should not allow ourselves to be cheated by a great experience by the attitude of the pacifists who weren't in it. Anyhow, I've purged my bosom of perilous stuff, and look forward to more creative work.

He adds:

I don't expect my novel to be treated with candour or fairness in England, but since I am making good rapidly in America, it leaves me more or less indifferent. However, I think you'll admit they'll have to take some notice of the novel. I suppose they'll say I imitated Remarque (excellent book) but I didn't read him until my own book was in type.

The enormous success of *All Quiet on the Western Front* had, however, prepared the public for *Death of a Hero* and Aldington sailed to fame and freedom on this new wave of "war books." He was never to be quite the same friend so far as I was concerned—not that his affection ever diminished, or that he grew distant and conceited, but I have experienced in other cases the desolation that popularity brings to friendship. We continued to exchange letters through 1930 and 1931, and there is much interesting discussion of the writing of the novels and short stories that followed *Death of a Hero*. There are no letters from 1932, but the correspondence revives again in 1933 to suddenly cease, for no apparent reason, with a letter written on the last day of 1934. Characteristically, it was a letter concerned about my own welfare—I was in temporary difficulties and Aldington, always kind and considerate to his friends, was trying to find me work with a London publisher.

I suspect that some letters must have been lost, for the next is dated more than eleven years later and came from Hollywood. It is a reply to one I had written from France, where I must have been on some official mission, and describes in mock-modest terms his new life in America. "I'm not much good at present—my salary is only $1,000 a week—but I have a kind of obstinate hankering to master this infernal trade at which nearly all English writers fail." I had asked him to come back to Europe and help in the work of cultural reconstruction after the war. "Your suggestion that I should return to Europe is rather like telling someone who, by dint of forethought and at some expense, has got a Pullman seat in a train de luxe to come and frolic in an Hommes 40 Chevaux 8. Merci, mon prince!" But the train de luxe did not get him anywhere. Eighteen months later he is writing:

These people degenerate on acquaintance . . . It is partly a difference of our temperaments, but partly also the result of residence, that I long ago ceased to expect any real contact or friendship with Americans, and lived with the landscape, the still extensive relics of primitive America. Rather as Lawrence did—except that I think his red Indians detestable and boring barbarians . . . I find myself hankering after France, but I am afraid of cold and food deficiencies for the child. What do you advise?

There is something pathetic about that question, and I no longer remember how I answered it. But as we know, he did eventually return to France, to live and work there in comparative modesty for the years that were left to him. France was always, I believe, his "spiritual home" and I think he was perhaps happier there than he had ever been in England or California.

I met him once or twice on his rare visits to London—the same gay but caustic Richard that I had first met in London forty years earlier. He urged me to come and visit him in Montpellier, but I was never able to go. His last letter was on the occasion of H. D.'s death, thanking me for the brief obituary I wrote in the *Times*. He was sad and disillusioned, talking of his old friends, Unkil Ez and Wyndham (Lewis) and described his new public in the U.S.S.R. "Personally, I think it an error to bother with the highbruffs . . . One should hope to reach the quiet 'reading man' and this new proletarian 'public' which will buy practically anything the booksellers shove at it."

That is sad. I prefer to think that Richard Aldington will be remembered by his "images"—images of war and of love. "After Two Years" is perhaps not specifically "imagist," but it is one of the most perfect lyrics in the English language.

> She is all so slight
> And tender and white
>   As a May morning
> She walks without hood
> At even. It is good
>   To hear her sing.
>
> It is God's will
> That I love her still
>   As he loves Mary.
> And night and day
> I will go forth to pray
>   That she love me.
>
> She is as gold
> Lovely, and far more cold.
>   Do thou pray with me,
> For if I win grace
> To kiss twice her face
>   God has done well to me.

Imagism was too limited in its ideals to survive as a poetic "movement," but it was a necessary stage in the evolution of English poetry, and Aldington, H. D., and Flint purified the literary atmosphere between 1910 and 1915 and prepared the way for the emergence of greater poets like Pound and Eliot. Perhaps the "Proem" which Aldington wrote in May, 1917, and placed at the beginning of his *Images of War* has some prophetic reference to his own career:

Out of this turmoil and passion,
This implacable contest,
This vast sea of effort,
I would gather something of repose,
Some intuition of the inalterable gods.
Some Attic gesture.

Each day I grow more restless,
See the austere shape elude me,
Gaze impotently upon a thousand miseries
and still am dumb.

Aldington did not remain "dumb," but his novels belong to the turmoil and passion of this age, and I prefer to think that he did, in his poetry, gather something of repose, some intuition of the inalterable gods.

C. P. Snow

Anyone in touch with twentieth-century literature knows Richard Aldington to be a writer of great gifts. You cannot pin him down as simply a "novelist" or "poet" or "critic"; he has already produced a large volume of work in each genre, much of it high and secure beyond controversy and depreciation. His achievement exists. He has followed his own course, and won his special place. His books are translated in over a dozen countries and are read all over the world.

You can read scarcely any of his work and remain indifferent. It produces that immediate *impact* which is a mark of the most intense writers. To get the most out of him, however, as with any writer, one needs to appreciate something beneath the first impact.

Let me begin with a commonplace. His writing is full of life. No one can read him for ten minutes without feeling a glow of power and vitality: a gusto both of the senses and of the mind: a natural, fluid ease with words: an

impression of someone seeing things ten times more vividly, and being both hurt and delighted ten times more
intensely, than most of us can ever manage.

"Full of life"—read *All Men Are Enemies* or the *Collected Poems* or *A Dream in the Luxembourg*. You will
feel that the phrase is *literally* true. The writing makes
you share an experience of life which has been unusually
complete; it glows with an appetite for living without
which the experience would have been dead. That warmth
and appetite for living shine through all his work: it is the
essence of his gift and vitalises everything he has to say.

Few writers have possessed such a zest for the variety
of experience in one man's life. I do not mean the observant
second-hand zest of Balzac—that is part of many writers'
equipment—but the actual passionate sense of one's own
pleasure and suffering as one goes alone through the world.
It is that sense which Aldington communicates with such
astonishing directness; he brings us nearer to another passionately felt experience than we thought we could ever
come.

This experience, as I have said, is wide as well as deep.
It is the life of "the here and now," as he calls it, the life
of the senses as well as of the emotions and the mind.
They all come home to us with the same absolute conviction and the certainty that we learn them at first hand.
They are expressed with the greatest power and *authority*.
The latter seems a curious word to use about a writer's
communication of his joy in immediate life; yet there is
no other which is quite so true. One never doubts the
genuineness nor the intensity of the experience. For this
man, one knows, it meant just that. A good many writers

have rhapsodised about the life of the senses. There is something forced and bogus about many of them. They are, so to speak, yodelling through their pince-nez. But no one could conceivably read Aldington and entertain such a doubt. His passions, his delights and his suffering, come to us as deeply and honestly as they did to himself. He is a man with an unusual capacity for them all. That is why he can enrich us with moments unlike those of anyone alive. That is why he can give us an intimation of experience so deep and yet immediate that we shall not see the world with quite the same eyes again.

Some people have, however, also felt a "bitterness" and a "harshness" which they allow to dominate their other responses to his writing. Of course, as soon as a critical slogan is put forward, it is the easiest thing in the world for it to spread. We are all more suggestible than we like to think. Fashions in criticisms are accordingly too easy to start, and dangerous when they are on the move. With the catchword "bitter" in the back of one's mind, one can read a book and find the bitterness in every line—and spare oneself the trouble of looking for anything else.

Something like that has often seemed to happen with Aldington's work. It is a pity. The bitterness is there all right. But it only predominates in one or two books, and in them is accompanied by much else. In everything he has written we ought to find many qualities far different and far more important. In order to get all we can from him, we need to understand the "bitterness," put it in its place, and see beneath it the particular conception of life, the particular kind of passion and sensitivity, of which it is only one result.

Most of his work is "personal" in the best sense. It is a passionately felt experience. To begin to understand it properly, I think we must understand some parts of his own personality; it is not by accident that often in his books, particularly in the prefaces, he has given some careful and deliberate self-revelations.

A certain kind of indrawn sensitivity, acting within a powerful and passionate nature, runs through much of his work. His books are full of people more than ordinarily sensitive and proud, more deeply humiliated, more easily subject to shame: proud individuals, aware of their own loneliness, desperately sensitive even to a hostile glance. But when these people of his can feel assured that they are liked, the barriers come down in an instant. Just as their pride was great, so is their happiness and surrender in love and friendship.

That acute inner sensitiveness lies behind a great deal of his writings, particularly in the novels. We understand them better, I think, as soon as we realise it; particularly if we also realise that it is coupled with force, authority and strength. That is, there is nothing passive about his sensitivity; if he feels suspicious of a hostile world, his impulse is to attack before he is himself attacked.

Often, then, he sees the world of human beings as remote, hostile and wounding. At other times, in friendship and essentially in love, he feels an ecstasy greater than the other enmity. It is from this other side, the happy side of his sensitivity, that he draws his hopes. He has called himself a "romantic idealist"—and that is absolutely true. He knows that he expects more of life than the mixture and contradictions of living can give. He believes in "in-

137

tegrity and comradeship," in his generation that "hoped much, strove honestly and suffered deeply": and most of all in his own romantic ideal of love, "the finer fuller life." "It is not only life with a woman he really loves, but the energy and beauty of existence which he wants to contribute to their joint possession. It is the life of the here and now, the life of the senses, the life of the deep instinctive forces."

He is a very learned man. He could be an eminent archaeologist if he wanted. He is a natural scholar (which may seem curious to some in the light of his other qualities). As a matter of fact, he has already produced a great many works of scholarship, which I can scarcely do more than enumerate here. Translations of Anyte of Tegeo, Meleager of Gadara, the Anacreontea (or Anacreon-like songs), Latin poets of the Renaissance—later collected together under the title of Medallions. Like all his translations, these are the work of an artist-scholar, and very beautiful.

Literary Studies and Reviews contains the essay, "An Approach to Marcel Proust," one of the first articles on Proust in English, and still full of enthusiasm and illumination. Incidentally, this article brings out one of Aldington's richest qualities; he has a devoted passion for art, and all his life he has been actively eager to search for and encourage a new talent. In one of the essays in *Artifex* he says: "I should have liked to live in the epoch of great artists, even if it were not granted to me to be the humblest amongst them. I should like to live in an age that was passionately creative, when society was as deeply stirred by high achievements of the creative spirit as it is now by trade, war and invention." That is utterly sincere. He can be a proud man in human relations; but before any sign of the creative spirit he will forego even his pride. Towards anything he can see as real talent, he is generous in a way few men could possibly achieve.

More learned works: *Voltaire*—the standard biography in English. *French Studies and Reviews, Four French Comedies of the Eighteenth Century* (note the introduction). *A Book of Characters,* a collection of descriptions of "character"-types from many languages. The *Dangerous Acquaintances* of Laclos, and the *Voyages* of Cyrano de Bergerac. The *Decameron* of Boccaccio. A translation of *Alcestis of Euripides. Fifty Romance Lyric Poems.* This selection and translation makes one of the most charming of his scholarly works. The Latin cultures have always moved him deeply, particularly that of mediaeval Provence; and in this translation he performed both a pious duty and a labour of love. To many—as to myself—about forty-five of these poems will come absolutely fresh. Translations of *Remy de Gourmont's Letters to the Amazon,* and *Selections from Remy de Gourmont.* The introductions to both these volumes are full of good things.

In these last books, we have seen him as a translator of other people's poems. It now remains to deal with his own. Of all his work, they seem to me the most perfect achievement. Before the war, he was beginning to be known as an imagist; between 1919 and 1929, the period in which he was largely busy with the works of learning and criticism, his reputation became considerable. The latter year saw the sudden and dramatic success of his first novel; since then he has paid to some extent the penalty of versatility—that is, success at one thing makes people irrationally depreciate one's accomplishment at another. Actually, his poetical output has gone steadily on, *A Dream in the Luxembourg, The Eaten Heart, Life Quest;* and then in 1937 *The Crystal World.* This last poem convinced many of what they had gradually been suspecting for some time: that Aldington has written some of the best love-poetry in English. Most of us are not over-willing to commit ourselves to a literary judgment on a contemporary; but that statement I would make myself without feeling that I was risking anything at all.

F. - J. Temple

A young French writer with a passion for D. H. Lawrence could hardly have wished anything better than to meet Richard Aldington, even had *Death of a Hero,* in the admirable translation by Henry D. Davray and Madeleine Vernon, not been among the books which dominated my adolescence. Besides, as a Frenchman and a modest student of English literature both, I was naturally familiar with his life of Voltaire, his translations of *Candide, Les Liaisons Dangereuses* and *Aurélia* and the *French Studies and Reviews* which reveal such an astonishing knowledge of our culture. I knew, too, that Richard Aldington had been the first in England to salute the genius of Marcel Proust. Finally, how could any poet have failed to value a meeting with one of the leaders of the "Imagist" movement which lifted English poetry from its torpor?

Miracles do happen. One day I discovered that Richard Aldington lived in the same town as myself; I even found that, in the Villa les Rosiers on the outskirts of Montpellier, he occupied the very room in which I was born. It was there that I went almost daily to see him until 1957 when he left the Midi to live in Alister Kershaw's cottage in the Cher.

For five years, Richard Aldington lived in Montpellier in almost total solitude. This man who loved France so deeply, who spoke our language faultlessly, who delighted in our finest wines, lived here like an outcast or, rather, like a retired Indian Army colonel in exile. The hostility he may have felt towards his own country, like the affection he undoubtedly felt for ours, was not reflected in a way of life any different to what it would have been in an English provincial town. I often saw his stalwart figure near the main post office where he went each day on the occasion of his solitary excursion and when I called at the Villa les Rosiers I was sure to hear the tapping of his typewriter which only stopped at noon and late at night.

To be quite candid, I think that Richard Aldington was a disappointed lover. Like his friend D. H. Lawrence, his love for England had been rejected and betrayed but, far from his native land, he remained utterly, almost desperately English.

The only moments of relaxation he allowed himself were on occasional Sundays with his daughter, Catherine, on the roads leading to the Camargue or the Languedoc *garrigue,* and I think I can say that I was then the only outsider to win his confidence and, eventually, to have the great happiness of becoming his friend. I need no more proof of this than the fact that he agreed to let me interview him for the French radio. Richard Aldington was, of all men, the most revolted by "publicity" and it need hardly be said that he felt supreme contempt for radio and television. I am certain that it cost him a great effort to come regularly to the studio and answer the (frequently naïve) questions I put to him. I still remember his extraordinary punctuality and his anxiety to be sure that he was giving me what I wanted.

It was a miserable time in his career. He was sick and I knew that his robust constitution had been undermined by the bitterness he felt ever since the English intellectuals, the Highbrows Associated, outraged by his book on the Colonel of Mecca, had first spewed up their venom and then ordained that Richard Aldington's name and work should never be mentioned. A boycott of mediocrities. It was not so much his physical self that suffered as his spirit, his love for life. Moreover, although he never said or hinted as much, he was painfully short of money. His royalties had dropped, since his books were rarely republished in England, while money due from sales in Russia (where, paradoxically, his works were tremendously successful) had not then come through. I was a helpless witness of his difficulties, which he bore with a truly lordly stoicism and dignity.

The five years he spent in Montpellier had a happy culmination, at any rate, when, shortly before he left, he was awarded the Prix Mistral whereby the Provençal writers paid homage to his book on the poet of Maillane. "Needless to say," the jury observed, "Richard Aldington does not see Provence in its 'folklore' aspects and his book takes us far from the vulgar commonplaces to which we have become all too accustomed . . . Among the many conventional studies of Mistral, only two or three works

143

of real value may be found. The most recent (last but not least) is Richard Aldington's. The jury is happy to pay tribute to this work and feels that it is by bestowing on this study of Mistral an exceptional award that it can best indicate the importance it attaches to those works imbued with the light of Provence."

This was some small solace at the time of Richard's departure from Montpellier. Thenceforward, he was to live at Maison Sallé, near Sury-en-Vaux, solitary as ever, but surrounded by the affectionate and practical care of the Berrichon peasants, unobtrusive but always present. I visited him several times there and we also met on his occasional visits to Aix-en-Provence or the Camargue. His health seemed to me, in these latter years, to be excellent: the air of the Berry had apparently restored the vigour which he had momentarily lost. That was enough to decide him to make a trip to Russia which he had always hitherto declined. His welcome was equal to the invitation itself. Readers came from many miles away to greet him and in Moscow he received tributes such as one might have hoped to find forthcoming in England where, however, the silence was unbroken. In Leningrad, from where I received his last card, he was enraptured by Voltaire's library; at Yasnaya Polyana, he visited Tolstoy's tomb. Richard had just turned seventy. It seemed reasonable to hope that he would start writing again and finish the monumental work he had begun on Balzac and which he had had to abandon or, at any rate, his translation of Flaubert's *Education Sentimentale*. A few of his books had reappeared in the United States. Perhaps a brighter future lay ahead.

In July of 1962 I wrote from Majorca where I was then staying to welcome him back to France. On 14 July I returned to Montpellier and, a few days later, received a telephone call from Alister Kershaw and learnt that Richard was dead.

It is so hard to believe that he is gone that I still sometimes find myself thinking I must write to him about one or another of the things that called forth those brilliant, sardonic replies. But the bitter loss is borne in on me again whenever I recall that July afternoon and the still body which I helped the village carpenter place in its coffin.

Now that the tributes of those who knew him are being assembled, I am made aware of the difficulty of discussing the man and his work. To have been, as I was, one of the small group who surrounded him in the last ten years of his life is at once a privilege and a source of bitterness. Those who can feel will understand how difficult I find it to speak of Richard Aldington and I have been able to do no more than set down the few words which friendship has clumsily dictated.

His death occasioned little interest in England and it was the provincial newspapers of the Berry which, with a touching awkwardness, first announced that Richard had died, with no orations, no procession, like a simple peasant.

Looking back, I cannot but recall the day when it fell to me to tell Richard of the sudden death of Roy Campbell. I remember how he mastered his emotion, how he sought to conceal his sorrow from Catherine, Alister and myself. We were unable to show the same courage when he, in turn, passed beyond that dark glass behind which the flesh becomes marble and memory grief.

Mikhail Urnov

Richard Aldington's earliest poems had only just appeared when he was first heard of in my country—although only by a very few people at that time. Even his name was pronounced differently in Russian then—"Aldington" instead of "Oldington," as we now pronounce it. The first time his name appeared was in an article by Zinaida Vengerova, entitled "English Futurists" (in the journal *Strelets,* Petrograd, 1915). Aldington was then forgotten.

Many years passed before he came into prominence. I heard of him in 1931 from the poet and translator Mikhail Zenkevich. Although we were keenly interested in English literature, which we read in the original, Aldington's name was at that time still unfamiliar and mysterious to me and many of my contemporaries. He had been mentioned in reviews a few times at the end of the twenties but had not aroused much interest. Mikhail Zenkevich, who sometimes also took part in discussions about poetry, knew his name well, and I still remember

him, turning over the pages of the *Publishers' Weekly*
and saying that a new edition of Aldington's first novel
had been published and that he absolutely must get hold
of it—it might be a very interesting book.

In the September issue of *Novy Mir* for 1931 appeared
a review entitled "English literature—a novel about Aunt
Sallies and the arrows of the spirit," which was devoted
to Richard Aldington and his *Death of a Hero*. The novel
was described as an important literary event. The review
was written by Evgeny Lann, who, in the following year,
published, in collaboration with A. V. Krivtsova, a translation of the novel (State Fiction Publications). Richard
Aldington immediately became popular in Russia. The
novel attracted the attention of writers, critics and a large
number of readers. "Have you read Richard Aldington's
book, *Death of a Hero?*" M. Gorky asked Konstantin
Fedin in a letter written on 29 March 1932—i.e. just after
the novel appeared. "Such an extremely harsh, angry and
'desperate' book; I would never have thought that the
English would produce a book like it!" M. Gorky regarded *Death of a Hero* not as an ordinary, everyday production, but as a symptomatic phenomenon. He returned
to the subject of the novel shortly afterwards, in an article
entitled "The old and the new man," which was published
simultaneously in *Pravda* and *Isvestia* on 27 April 1932,
and also in the *New Statesman and Nation*. He wrote,
"In the country where once the misty good humour of
the optimist Dickens veiled the healthy criticism of Thack-
eray, it is not long since we heard the gloomy voice of
T. Hardy, and now it has become possible to write such
harsh books, full of sinister despair, as R. Aldington's

Death of a Hero." (See the thirty-volume Collected Works of M. Gorky, Moscow, Goslitizdat, 1953, Vol. 26, page 282.)

Soviet critics and readers did not consider *Death of a Hero* as an isolated phenomenon—they read it along with Remarque's *All Quiet on the Western Front* and Hemingway's *Farewell to Arms,* and instinctively thought of it together with them. Many years afterwards, Soviet readers, meeting Aldington, asked him, "What general features, in your opinion, have your books in common with Hemingway's?" Aldington appeared embarrassed and at a loss. It is, however, easy to understand why this and similar questions were asked—one only has to take into account the fact that we were reading books by various writers from various countries at the same time— authors who wrote under the pressure of the same painful reflections and who foresaw the same threatening events in the future. It could hardly have been a coincidence that Aldington, Remarque and Hemingway, who fought in the First World War and experienced its tragedy, published anti-war novels in the same year—1929. They wrote their impassioned books about events that had happened more than ten years before, and they were urged on by fresh events—the impending threat of fascism and the danger of another world war.

It was partly due to the open-mindedness of the reading public and their broad outlook that they were not bewildered when, in *Death of a Hero,* refined taste and delicate feeling for elegance came up against despairing harshness. And their perplexity naturally decreased when the writer turned to the story of the dramatic life of George

Winterbourne. They took up this subject involuntarily; the book gripped them because of its subject matter—not because of its plot but because of its portrayal of a mental and moral atmosphere, its treatment of psychological problems, and especially its moral questioning and its protest, which are due to the need for a free and harmonious life. This was close to the traditions of Russian literature and to the spiritual sympathies of the Soviet reader—it increased his interest in following the hero's short-lived destiny. He sympathised sincerely with George Winterbourne's attempts to extricate himself from the closed circle, and, following the author's indications, he tried to explain for himself a good code of personal honesty, and what were the forces by which he was doomed to torment, sapping his will to live and impelling him towards disaster. The reader felt that the humanistic idea was clearly perceptible through the harshness, anger and sinister despair.

When I met Richard Aldington, I asked him to read something out of *Death of a Hero,* so that I could record it on tape and preserve it. I handed him the book, and he thought for a minute, turned over a few pages, and, it seemed to me, in a good-natured, willing way and with a desire to stress a mood that was not just a transient thing, he read, with impressive clarity and controlled passion, an extract from the dedication to Halcott Glover—the last two paragraphs, which follow the words "Through a good many doubts and hesitations and changes I have always preserved a certain idealism. I believe in men, I believe in a certain fundamental integrity and comradeship, without which society could not endure," and end "I believe that all we claim is that we try to say what appears to be the truth, and that we are not afraid either to contradict ourselves or to retract an error." These words can be heard throughout the novel. Even at my first reading, they struck me, and I am sure that they impress any Soviet reader similarly. A reader who studied George Winterbourne carefully could not fail to notice that a new feeling of humanity—a special feeling, hitherto unknown to the hero—was coming to life in him, and that this feeling was reinforced by the devotion expressed in these words. In the first place, the war makes the hero, who is a bourgeois intellectual and an artist and aesthete, feel the falsity of his position in relation to ordinary people. "With them to the end"—that is the new, vitally important aspiration which has arisen within him. The bankruptcy of the old ideas and obsolete social principles seemed to him to underline the failure of egoistic, individualist morality, which rested on the basis of such principles.

The second edition of *Death of a Hero* came out in 1935, with a foreword by Ivan Anisimov, now director of the M. Gorky Institute of World Literature (U.S.S.R. Academy of Sciences). At that time Anisimov was in personal contact wtih Romain Rolland, Theodore Dreiser, and other well-known people, and he initiated the publication of many outstanding books by Western authors. He was an intellectual of genuine Soviet roots, and he studied carefully the processes which took place in the formation of an intellectual milieu in other countries. Recommending Aldington's book to the Soviet reader, he wrote:

Aldington who is one of the most cultured and most talented writers in England today and an excellent expert on modern literature and a most penetrating critic . . . has collected a great deal of material which bears witness to the desperate crisis of contemporary writing. He has even gone further, and linked "the spiritual crisis" and the increasing corruption of society. . . . This crisis showed the bankruptcy of capitalism so clearly that its enmity to true culture has become clear to anyone who had not lost the ability to think honestly. It was particularly easy for a man like Aldington, who has translated Euripides and Anacreon with great delicacy of understanding, who has made a profound study of Voltaire and the Latin poets of the Renaissance, and who has a profound feeling for historical tradition, to come to the conclusion that contemporary "civilisation" was barbarism. All that was needed was to make a comparison with the past—from the great achievements of human culture to the cynical grimaces and convulsions of dying art, to the "concavisms" ironically described in the novel is such a long step as to give one every reason to reflect. And Aldington writes about the "decline of the West" directly, without reserve, mercilessly. This, indeed, is part of the power of this exceptional novel. It is because of this that Aldington has been able to portray with such freedom, such passion and such veracity what Rolland in his day called "the fair on the square"—the monstrously hideous world of pseudo-civilisation, the cloaca of "the prostitution of the mind." Everything Aldington has written in this field is excellent—genuine and very bitter realism. We may say that Aldington comes very close to the line beyond which begins a completely new field of conceptions, values and relations. He has reached the "limit" attainable by a writer within the confines of bourgeois "respectability." One step further and Aldington would have had to cross the line dividing him from the new world. . . . In his novel Aldington has done a great deal in the sphere in which the work of the best "masters of culture" who had broken with capitalism was developing—but he has still not "decided." He is waiting while he "thinks it over," and we do not know when he will have finished.

In any case, "decision" is as necessary as air for the creative work of this talented writer.

I have quoted these lengthy extracts because I consider them extremely revealing. They contain an evaluation of the novel and of the writer's talent, his social outlook and his psychological condition—a definite clear-cut evaluation, full of profound feeling and forward-looking. The extracts also show the sympathy and expectation with which our critics of that period regarded Aldington.

In the same year—1935—the novel *The Colonel's Daughter* appeared in a Russian translation. The critics thought it "very interesting in its own way"; they thought the bitter story of the unhappy Georgie Smithers excellent in its way but considered that the whole book was "a trivial story by comparison with the massive scale of *Death of a Hero*." General opinion, however, inclined—as it still does—towards the belief that it is one of Aldington's best books, coming after *Death of a Hero* and *All Men are Enemies*.

All Men are Enemies appeared in Russia in 1937 in two different translations. At the beginning it had a varied reception. Some press reviews were sharply critical—for example, a review in *Literaturnaja Gazeta* by the eminent writer, the late Yury Olesha. Comparing the new novel with *Death of a Hero,* this reviewer saw it as a retreat and a decline. The novel withstood criticism, however. The rhapsodical account of how feelings are awakened and how they mature, the hero's spiritual searching, the dramatic love story, the writer's sincere, painful confessions, his exposure of social injustice, the robbery of wartime and the predatoriness of the postwar period—all this attracted the Soviet reader, as it still does, and it is given its due by literary experts, although they consider *Death of a Hero* the best of Aldington's works. Still, a great many readers would put *All Men are Enemies* first among his novels. In the same year Russian readers were introduced to some of Richard Aldington's poems. Nine of his poems, translated by Mikhail Zenkevich, appeared in *An Anthology of New English Poetry,* published by the Leningrad branch of the Goslitizdat.

In 1938, in a journal entirely devoted to foreign literature, appeared *Very Heaven* (*Internatsional'naja Literatura,* 1938, No. I). It received a lot of attention in the press, and was subsequently published in two separate editions. "The sincerity and literary honesty of Aldington make *Very Heaven* an interesting—even an exciting—book," wrote the experienced critic V. Druzin in a controversial review entitled "The living writer and the hypocritical critic" (in the Leningrad journal *Rezets,* 1938, No. 17, September). He attacked "the hypocritical mien and the lecturing forefinger" of some reviewers who wrote about *Very Heaven,* and he especially praised an article on the novel by the writer Andrey Platanov (in the journal *Literaturny kritik,* 1938, No. 5).

I fully agree with D. G. Zhantieva, a great admirer of Aldington's talent, who knew him personally and has written about him several times. She recently pointed out (in the journal *Soviet Literature,* 1962, No. 12) that about

153

that time Richard Aldington was almost the favourite contemporary English writer among Russians.

I remember that in 1938, at a conference for postgraduate students held at the Moscow Institute of History, Philosophy and Literature, on foreign writers who had opposed reaction and its most extreme expressions—Nazism and Fascism—I read a paper on the work of Richard Aldington. This is another indication of the widespread interest in Aldington among all sorts of people and their deep appreciation of him and his progressive civic outlook.

Not one of Richard Aldington's books has failed to attract notice by our critics. A booklet by C. P. Snow entitled *Richard Aldington* also received attention. Moreover, even in the grimmest period of the war Aldington's literary work continued to arouse interest. In 1942, for example, appeared a review by Mikhail Zenkevich of the anthology compiled by Richard Aldington, *Poetry of the English-Speaking World* (*Internatsional'naja Literatura*, 1942, No. I). The reviewer referred to the book as "the fullest and one of the best anthologies of poetry in the English language." I agree with him. When you open Aldington's anthology, you know that you will find in it not only the poems usually considered "the best" but also —and this is less common—the poems that you personally like.

There was another great surge of interest in Richard Aldington, in Russia, after the publication, in 1955, of his book *Lawrence of Arabia*. Soviet critics gave due recognition to the worth of this carefully reasoned study of the British intelligence agent, which exposes the legend of the

154

"national hero" put into circulation and still maintained by the colonialists.

In 1956 a short article of mine entitled "Richard Aldington and his books" was published in the journal *News*. Aldington wrote to me about it. I replied, and a correspondence between us began, which went on until a few days before his death. I am sure that these letters of Aldington's are not only of personal interest. For the moment, I shall only say that Richard Aldington was extremely upset by persecution and lying propaganda. On 27 December 1956 he wrote to me, "I was asked to write the biography and I wrote it in accordance with the facts I discovered. But it appeared that 'Colonel' Lawrence (a temporary Foreign Office official with honorary military rank to protect him from conscription!) was and still is a 'national hero,' not of the nation, but of the upper class clique and the Foreign and Colonial Office, plus Sir Winston and the people who call themselves 'the Establishment.' They couldn't answer my facts, so the newspaper hacks were put up to abuse me and now to boycott me. It was even worse in U.S.A. . . . I have letters from British generals and officers from the Middle East saying I am right about Lawrence, but no English or American periodical will publish them!" In a letter written on 6 September 1960 he wrote, "There is a successful play on the life of T. E. Lawrence by Terence Rattigan in London—and it is a tissue of falsehood. Of course it is all propaganda, and I was to be starved into submission for resisting it." And again, in a letter written on 15 December 1960. "Your support of my work kept up my morale when the official

Anglo-American propaganda machine was trying to reduce me to ruin and beggary."

There is a curious fact which Richard Aldington told his Soviet friends when he was in Moscow. In 1958 I sent him a volume of the *History of English Literature* published by the U.S.S.R. Academy of Sciences, in which there was a chapter about his work. Aldington asked an acquaintance of his who knew Russian to look over this chapter. The acquaintance began by looking up Aldington's name in the index, and said that Aldington had been misled by his Soviet friends—there was nothing about him in the book that had been sent to him. Then everything was explained—as I said already, in Russian the name "Aldington" is transliterated "Oldington." This "detail," however, was indicative of the atmosphere of mistrust which was not easily surmounted, even for Richard Aldington.

In 1959, a newly edited version of *All Men are Enemies* was published—the first publication after a long interval. It was published by Goslitizdat, in the series *The Foreign XXth Century Novel,* which is very popular among Soviet readers. In 1961, the same publishing house published, in the same series, a new translation of *Death of a Hero,* and the Foreign Literature Publishing House produced a collection of Aldington's stories entitled *Farewell to Memories*. The contents and title of the collection were approved by the author. This was the first time that an almost complete edition of the writer's stories appeared in Russia; a few stories which are below the general standard are not included in this collection. The novel *Death*

of a Hero was also published in English by the Foreign
Languages Publishing House.

Over thirty years, large numbers of copies of Richard
Aldington's works have been printed. In 1935, *Death of a
Hero* and in 1937 *All Men are Enemies* ran to 10,000
copies. In the second half of the fifties and at the beginning of the sixties, the situation changed dramatically.
The number of copies printed of the 1961 edition of
Death of a Hero was ten times as large (100,000 copies).
All Men are Enemies ran to 225,000 copies (Goslitizdat)
and was also published in Smerdlovsk, by a local publishing house which printed around 100,000 copies. These
books did not lie round in the bookshops—they were sold
literally in a few days, and now it is impossible to find
them in the shops—not one reader has offered to sell to
a second-hand bookseller, evidently because people do not
want to part with them. When Richard Aldington's
friend, Mr. Alister Kershaw, asked me to send him old
Russian editions of the writer and I tried to get them from
the second-hand booksellers, I was told, "There are neither
old ones nor new ones to be had."

It was towards evening on a warm clouded summer's
day when at last we saw Richard Aldington. On 23 June
1962, accompanied by his daughter Catherine, he stepped
out of the plane at the Sheremetevo Airport, as the guest
of the Soviet Writers' Union. We—the group of his
friends who had gathered to meet him—recognised him
at once, as soon as he began to come down the steps.

A few press photographs were taken while we were
warmly shaking hands, and others later on the journey to
Moscow—one particularly successful, memorable photo-

graph showed Richard Aldington alone, and another with his daughter, against a background of the light-coloured trunks of the Russian birches. Then there was the first, gay meal at the Pekin Hotel, a trip round both old and new Moscow, and three weeks in the Soviet Union. Richard Aldington met various people whom he wished to see and visited Moscow, Leningrad and Yasnaya Polyana, met publishers and fellow-writers, interviewed journalists, although at first he had not intended to, and even appeared on television when he was in Leningrad in a broadcast for young people (this, too, he had not meant to do). Aldington's meetings with his readers were impressive—a large meeting of readers was held in the Foreign Language Library in Moscow, and he met individual readers in the street, in hotels, theatres and museums.

Richard Aldington celebrated his seventieth birthday while he was in Moscow. He was touched by the attention paid him by anonymous readers who brought him flowers and went away without being observed as they did not wish to tire him. Aldington himself told about this, and particularly about a young chauffeur who did not want to disturb the writer but was very anxious to see him. He travelled from outside Moscow, and sat waiting for two hours in the hotel while Aldington was resting.

Aldington was moved by the celebrations for his seventieth birthday. A reception was arranged by the Soviet Writers' Union, and was held in the writers' club in Vorovsky Street. At this reception, Richard Aldington said, "Several times in my life I have suffered from the literary fraternity, and I am accustomed to shrugging my shoulders in answer to insults and pinpricks. Here, in the

Soviet Union, for the first time in my life I have met with extraordinary warmth and attention. This is the happiest day in my life. I shall never forget it."

Whoever I spoke to about Richard Aldington—writers, critics, publishers, or readers who had an opportunity to make the acquaintance of our guest—they all spoke about him in the warmest terms. He left behind him the happiest memories of his sincerity, a reserved feeling of personal worth, humility, and that fundamental integrity in which he believed so strongly, and all this, together, made up a personality of great attraction.

Every writer has his own leading idea, his own sentiment, an idea which is a passion that goes through and through his work. It may be an intuitive idea or entirely conscious, an all-embracing idea or confined to a particular aspect of his thought, it may flare up and die down, grow, undergo change, but it must be there, so that both great and trifling impressions of life may take their place in the literary whole. However many-sided such passionate ideas may be, they must be humanitarian ideas if his literary work is to be sincere. This is their whole meaning and purpose, and this is their unifying principle.

In one of his conversations, Aldington defined the underlying idea of his creative work in the short and, at first sight, somewhat mysterious statement, "To live here and now." But in these words was passionate conviction—the humanist challenge can be heard in them. His words clearly indicate distrust in any sort of demagogic promises and exhortations and disapproval of anything that takes away from man his earthly happiness. These words show how devoted the writer was to humanist thinking and that he accepted the demands of humanism in our day—the belief that people want to live as human beings, that they have a right to do so and that it is objectively possible.

Richard Aldington was greatly interested in the problems of a harmonious personality and harmonious relations between people. He begins by looking at the individual man and with sincere interest he studies his feelings—a complex and difficult field of study. Then he gradually widens his circle of observation, and watches to see how, in the life of the individual, close, intricate links are forged between him and the external world, and how all feelings, even intimate ones, depend on the social form of his life. Having begun with an analysis of natural feelings, the writer turns to examine social relations. Having spoken his exultant word in defence of life, he also had to attack passionately whatever leads to its impoverishment and encourages death. Following this train of thought, he came to the conclusion that "the era of private property" was drawing to its end and that "some form of socialism is inevitable." He did not take the final step, "did not cross the line," and this is dramatically reflected in his work and in his life.

I have sometimes been disturbed at the thought of my sharp reproofs, my constant criticism of anarchic individualism, from the influence of which Richard Aldington could not free himself. But I could not imagine any other form in which I could survey the life and work of a writer I valued and respected, and I remembered his final words from his dedication to Halcott Glover. I spoke about this to Richard Aldington, and I gained the impression that he was prepared to "acknowledge his mistakes." Even earlier, judging from his letters, I thought that, in spite of his physical weakness and the depression he felt as a result of the atmosphere of open and calculated hostility, Richard Aldington wanted to return to active creative work. "Ah, if only I could write as Anatole France did!" he said in one of his letters—i.e., with such conviction, with such a subtle combination of intelligence, sarcasm and humanity. Aldington's unsatisfied longing can be seen in this remark. I saw him start when, at the U.S.S.R. Academy of Sciences Publishing House, he was given a catalogue of the "Voltaire Library" (which he later visited in Leningrad), and he once said that he would perhaps return to creative work and would write a novel, come back to the Soviet Union, settle by the sea, and write.

Richard Aldington has always been accepted in Russia, and still is, as a many-sided figure, a rounded personality. Articles have been written about him as a poet and a novelist, a translator and a critic, a man and a writer; the content of his works has been discussed and also their form, his works as a whole and individual books, and articles, studies, reviews and notices about him have appeared in works published in Moscow and Leningrad, in journals and in newspapers published in other cities. Papers have been read about him, lectures given, and students have written essays on him. His books have reached every part of our large country. And—what is even more important—his books are read. Our older and younger generations know Richard Aldington. He lives in our memory.

Alec Waugh

I had not seen Richard Aldington since 1938. But when I read of his death last year I felt that I had lost one of my best friends. I had met him first in the spring of 1919 at one of the bachelor parties that Harold Monro used to give at The Poetry Bookshop. Richard was six years older than I, but we met as equals and contemporaries as two ex-subalterns back from the wars who had won their spurs in the literary arena, he as a poet, I as a novelist. We had a great deal in common. An acquaintance soon became a friend. That spring his poem *Reverie* appeared in *The English Review*. I greatly admired it. The pleasure his poetry gave me was an added bond between us.

Reverie describes how a soldier in a quiet part of the line in France broods over his wife in England. Written in rhythmed verse, it is tender, wistful, nostalgic, uncomplaining. I still think it is a very lovely poem. I still think he is one of the best English war poets. There was no savagery, no resentment, not even the sting of satire in his war poems. They were love poems, rather than war poems.

He was at his best when he wrote of love. "Have I written too much or not enough of love?" he asks in *Epilogue,* one of his most quoted poems. In such moods as *The Colonel's Daughter* and *All Men Are Enemies* and in his biography of T. E. Lawrence, he was angry, resentful, bitter. But there was no spleen, no venom in *A Dream in the Luxembourg* and *The Crystal World.* Sensually, happily fulfilled, he wrote out of his memories of delight.

In his friendships he was the same person that he was in his poems. In his social contacts he displayed none of the ill temper that marked and I think marred so much of his prose writing. His talk did not scintillate, but it was sound, varied, entertaining. It stimulated talk in others. Parties went better for his presence. He enjoyed good company and good wine. I have never heard him speak spitefully or enviously of another writer.

He leaves to those few of his old friends who are still alive a store of fond and grateful memories, and to the public a body of poetry which surely will survive "the chances and changes" of our distracted day.

Henry Williamson

In the spring of 1949, my wife and I motored from Norfolk to the Riviera, to stay for our honeymoon at Le Lavandou, where Richard Aldington was then living. This visit was proposed by a young friend of Aldington's, who had come from Australia to meet three writers, among others—Roy Campbell, Richard Aldington and myself.

Alister Kershaw I had already met in Devon. We had bathed and walked together, and motored in my 1938 2-litre Aston-Martin, and when he had gone back to London we had kept in touch. I already knew, and greatly liked, Roy Campbell; and it was during an evening at the Savage Club in London that Alister declared that I must meet Richard, who had returned from the United States after the war and rented a villa on a hillside above the coast east of Toulon.

It was the first time I had motored in France since the war of 1914–18 with its occasional lorry-hops. From battered Calais the road ran to Arras and Cambrai, and on through Beauvais to Paris, where we arrived in the early morning, and then on to Fontainebleau and the route to the south. We were in no hurry; the weather was fine, leaves were out on the trees, it was April—down the Rhône valley, our first *virages,* and in the evening Le Lavandou. Alister Kershaw had found us a room in the Sablons d'Or, where we were to have our meals. Nightingales were singing on the hills, our host had a gramophone amplifier in his vinery, where we sat and drank champagne with the moon shining through the glass overhead. I had never been so happy—Chopin, moon, nightingales: all the compost of the past, memories of boyhood before 1914, of the war and nightingales in the Ancre valley and under Messines hill, and before the *Siegfried Stellung,* all poetry and beauty seemed to have become real at last upon the shores of that clear, tideless sea.

Aldington was a shy man, I knew; but soon it was plain that he was more guarded than shy. He was hospitable and kind, in a remote way; he had been hurt in his early years, one saw that in much of his writings. And having lived out of England for so long, he had lived under the pain of his early memories. I recalled how he had written to me in 1930, when I had published a book about walking over the battlefields of Flanders, Picardy, and Artois, and the *Times Literary Supplement* had quoted part of the preface wherein I had written that my father had, in 1919, been angered when I had said that the Germans were brave soldiers, and generally had fought cleanly and as courageously as the British; he had very nearly called me a traitor, being much agitated and still hurt by the war propaganda. I was sorry I had written that passage to convey a criticism which had been based on imperfect sympathy: for my father had been a special constable all during the war, and had been blown up by a Zeppelin bomb and covered by powdered glass; but more injurious than that had been the lack of bodily action on the battlefield which had released mental tensions among the combatants, and given them a wider vision with the hopes of a League of Nations which would make war a thing of the past.

This I wrote to Aldington, and had no further communication with him until, following another bitter war, I was sitting in his villa among the aromatic shrubs under the hot sun of April and May, determined not to speak of my own writings or air any opinions, but to listen to him and learn about the Côte d'Azur and its wild life, about which he had a great knowledge, particularly of butterflies.

His face lit up when he talked as he told me about his boyhood in Kent, but at other times he was inclined to be bitter when he spoke about England. Having been away, except for brief visits, since the late twenties, his mind was still of the twenties; preserved like whisky kept in a glass bottle, in which it is unable to mature. Kept in the wood, it loses by evaporation and absorption, thus it matures. Of course I did not tell him this; it would have been not only tactless but unkind. He still suffered those strains and hopeless flingings-away that most of the immature survivors of the infantry war—we who had gone out almost without having shaved—had suffered in those early postwar years; the barbed wire was still encircling his heart, the iron fragments of shells in the bone of his skull. But of course one knew that was only part of the story; for a division within the spirit occurs in childhood, and the war was but a visible extension of that split between a child's parents. The lonely, rebellious soldier was the lonely, unhappy child, who in periods of frightful misery occurring occasionally among normally happy comrades bears the entire war upon his shoulders, and if he survives may be upset or driven into the solitudes of his own soul until, by a miracle, true love comes to dissolve the strictures of the past.

Richard, one divined, was still a lonely man, bound by invisible fetters forged in the shadows of childhood. Proserpine had not come to him, through the shades of a mortified past. Gradually he revealed himself to me, a youth with the love of the true England, its countryside, orchards, and white cliffs of Dover, the pebbly shores and the racing tides of the Channel—memories overcast by the petrifaction of past despairs. I was told that his mother had been a strong, self-willed woman who had dominated both a gentle husband and a gentle son. This, it seemed to me later on, was the key to his gradual dislike turning to contempt when he learned that T. E. Lawrence's mother had ruled her sons and their father with a self-will tautened at times to fury by her inner unresolved problem: she a Calvinist, believing literally in the Bible as God's word. "God forgives the sinner: but never the sin."

We returned to Le Lavandou in 1949, in the early autumn. Richard still lived in his villa, but his wife had returned to live in England. His love was for his daughter, a young girl who appeared to be living a life of her own, living in the mind, as indeed, we all come to live sooner

167

or later. Catherine was devoted to her father. She had the gift of composure, a perception above the ordinary, and was among other things an enduring swimmer.

Alister Kershaw had helped Richard greatly by his coming. He looked after the poet's correspondence; he was a courier between London and Le Lavandou, proposing books which Richard might care to consider writing, and arranging terms. For once a worthy young man had been able to prove his worth.

I have many letters from Richard, the majority of them discussing a new work he was preparing, a biography of T. E. Lawrence. I had met Lawrence in the late twenties, and liked him greatly; I owed much to him for encouragement and criticism. At the same time, while I saw how the book was to progress—the letters from expressing wonder eventually became scornful and then dismissive of the "hero"—I did not allow this to alter my affection for "Riccardo."

Many times my friend suggested that I should leave my work—which was being written continuously, often seven days a week for months on end, sometimes starting at 3 A.M., for I was sleepless and worried about my ability to carry out what had been planned to be started in 1929 and had been delayed by circumstances until 1949—and have a holiday with him at Montpellier, or later still in the Cher where Alister had a house. Alas, I did not go to visit him; then one day I heard he was dead; and later still I found myself alone, and the future uncertain, or rather it now seems to be as certain as that of my dear friend of Le Lavandou days.

Dilyara Zhantieva

To several generations of Soviet readers the name of Richard Aldington means a great deal. That is why the loss of a great writer who in his best works strove for man's dignity so deeply moves them. We know the struggle was not easy in the literary situation in Britain after the First World War. It saw the rise of modernist literature whose exponents tended to explain social calamities by the baseness of human nature. War manifested man's bestial instincts and its destructive power would put an end to civilisation, they affirmed; they proclaimed the writer's right to be irresponsible, to escape from reality. Richard Aldington opposed these trends, most clearly expressed in James Joyce's *Ulysses*. "Man is not like that," he declared in his review of the novel and he cited many instances of true comradeship, unassuming heroism and self-sacrifice by ordinary people he met in the trenches during the war.

His first novel, *Death of a Hero,* is one of the most

powerful anti-war novels, winning renown far beyond England's borders. Those of us who read it when it first appeared in 1929 were greatly impressed. We perceived its passionate protest against man's degradation, against war's senseless cruelty, against the lies and hypocrisy of those who unleashed the war. The novel, marking an important stage in Aldington's development as a writer, was anticipated by earlier poetry—the *Images of War* cycle (1919), conveying an awareness of the monstrous unnaturalness of war, and the long poem *A Fool i' the Forest* (1925), condemning the venality, lies and pretense of the modern world. These works, reflecting all he thought and felt about the war, contrast sharply with his early poetry: Aldington began his literary career as a representative of the modernist trend of Imagism, which was far removed from life. Even then it is true there were many signs that he felt cramped in the Imagist framework. His front-line experience, realisation of the falsity of jingo slogans and of the callousness of the war machine—all this forced him to reassess his view of prewar England, to hate the hypocrisy of fair phrases used to cover foul deeds.

His best works, written in the twenties and thirties, deal with war and its consequences—the novels *Death of a Hero* (1929), *The Colonel's Daughter* (1931), *All Men are Enemies* (1933), *Women Must Work* (1934), *Very Heaven* (1937), and collections of stories *Roads to Glory* (1930) and *Soft Answers* (1932). These were books about the maimed lives of men who had lived through the hardships of the front, but for whom the postwar world had no place. Aldington also portrayed in masterly fashion the complacency of those the war had made rich, the spiritual wasteland of the "gilded youth" and of the addicts of modernist art.

For lengthy periods of time he lived away from England, leaving it for good at the end of 1938. During his residence in the United States (1938–1946) and in France (1946–1962) he wrote only one novel, *The Romance of Casanova* (1946), and was engaged mainly in translation, compiling anthologies, writing books of history, biography, literary criticism. When a Soviet reader asked him during his visit to the Soviet Union about the later period of his writing, he showed exceptional honesty and a strict attitude towards a writer's duty in his reply. He said that the Second World War had brought about great changes in the world and in Britain in particular; he could not write about the new problems and motives of behaviour of people if he did not feel he could penetrate to the heart of things and this was absolutely necessary for a writer. A work of art can be created only when one feels one must write. (It should be noted, however, that he said in another conversation that he might perhaps write another novel.) He also made an important further point that in his biographical works he followed the same principle as in writing novels: respect for the facts, for the truth of life.

To the end of his days Aldington retained the integrity of a great artist and strove to serve truth.

He condemned the exponents of modernist art who attempted to "stand aloof from good and ill," who treated the masses with contempt and wrote for a narrow circle of people. *"Les beaux arts,"* he wrote not so long ago to the author of this article, "are arts partly of expression and partly of communication, but essentially of communication. The artist has no right to put himself above society." Those who proclaim the theory of "art for the happy few . . . don't know how to move great audiences as for example Balzac, Dickens and Tolstoy. . . . In the modern world there is no excuse for ignorance, and the claim that 'the artist' works only 'to express himself' and has no responsibility to society is sheer insolence." In connexion with his criticism of the ugly and incomprehensible works of abstract painting, which enjoy the favour of rich patrons, Aldington wrote: ". . . it is not millionaires who need art—they value it as a possession—but the people who are starved of beauty." Richard Aldington condemned those who for the sake of the "latest fashion" professed scorn for the heritage of culture. Can one possibly "reject the art of earlier great artists," he asked in one of his letters, "as our impertinent young men here want to do?"

On arriving in our country Aldington met true admirers of his work. Many Soviet readers know his works in the original and in translation. Recently there have been new Soviet editions of *All Men Are Enemies* (1959) and *Death of a Hero* (1961). The latter novel was published in English by the Foreign Languages Publishing House. A collection of the short stories *Farewell to Memories* (1961) has been published in Russian for the first time. It includes stories from the collections *Roads to Glory* and *Soft Answers*. As in the thirties, publication of Aldington's works in Russian was marked by reviews and articles in many Soviet newspapers and magazines.

Why do Soviet readers love Aldington? I think the

right answer was given at his meeting with readers in the State Library of Foreign Literature: his works are valued because he puts into them all the power of his soul. The many readers' letters he received from all parts of the Soviet Union showed they love him for his sincerity, closeness to readers, for expressing himself in his favourite characters. "We felt a lump in our throat when we read *Death of a Hero,* we did not know one could write like that about war," Karaganda engineers, who had fought in the Second World War, wrote to Aldington. Those who discussed *All Men Are Enemies* in their letters were moved by its portrayal of real love, by its pure attitude towards woman and respect for her. Some readers travelled to Moscow specially to see Aldington—a driver from the Moscow region, an engineer-translator from Rybinsk . . .

Richard Aldington was profoundly moved by the attitude of Soviet readers towards him. During the celebration on the occasion of his seventieth birthday at the Soviet Writers' Union ("the happiest day in my life," he called it) Aldington said that in his literary career he had received slaps and blows and had grown used to react to them with a mere shrug of the shoulders. For the first time in his life—in the Soviet Union—he had found warmth and attention. "I shall never forget it," he said.

Asked by a Soviet journalist what wishes he would like to convey to the Soviet people, Aldington recalled the caption to a drawing by Jean Effel on the cover of an issue of *Foreign Literature* magazine and said: "Peace, bread and roses." In a Leningrad television programme for youth Aldington noted Soviet youth's love of art, their care for their cultural heritage and said that he wished them to make the best use of the opportunities their country offers them.

Richard Aldington will always be remembered by Soviet readers as a great humanist writer and a man of integrity.

A CHRONOLOGICAL CHECK LIST OF

THE BOOKS BY RICHARD ALDINGTON

prepared by PAUL SCHLUETER

Aside from two items which first appeared in French and German, before any subsequent publication in English, this check list is confined to the first British and American editions, in the order in which they appeared. A few items were published in English but were issued prior to any publication in England or America; in such cases, the first publication as well as the first British and American editions are listed. Variant titles are indicated by indentation. Annotations are by ALISTER KERSHAW.

POETRY

Images (1910–1915). London: The Poetry Bookshop, 1915.
  Images Old and New. Boston: The Four Seas Co., 1916.
Reverie. A Little Book of Poems for H. D. Cleveland: The
  Clerk's Press, 1917.
The Love of Myrrhine and Konallis, and Other Prose Poems.
  Cleveland: The Clerk's Press, 1917.
————. Chicago: Pascal Covici, 1926.
Images of War. A Book of Poems. Westminster: C. W. Beaumont, 1919.
————. London: George Allen and Unwin Ltd., 1919 [expanded ed.].
————. Boston: The Four Seas Co., 1921.

Images of Desire. London: Elkin Mathews, 1919.

Images. London: The Egoist Ltd., 1919.

War and Love (1915–1918). Boston: The Four Seas Co., 1919.

The Berkshire Kennet. London: The Curwen Press, 1923.

Collected Poems, 1915–1923. London: George Allen and Unwin Ltd., 1923.

Exile and Other Poems. London: George Allen and Unwin Ltd., 1923.

A Fool i' the Forest. A Phantasmagoria. London: George Allen and Unwin Ltd., 1924.

Hark the Herald. Paris: The Hours Press, 1928.

The Eaten Heart. Chapelle-Reanville, Eure, France: The Hours Press, 1929.

——. London: William Heinemann Ltd., 1931.

Collected Poems. London: George Allen and Unwin Ltd., 1929.

Movietones. Invented and Set Down by Richard Aldington, 1928–1929. Privately printed, 1932.

Love and the Luxembourg. New York: Covici, Friede, Inc., 1930.

A Dream in the Luxembourg. London: Chatto and Windus, 1930.

(Also published in Czech and French.)

The Poems of Richard Aldington. Garden City, N.Y.: Doubleday, Doran & Co., Inc., 1934.

Life Quest. London: Chatto and Windus, 1935.

——. Garden City, N.Y.: Doubleday, Doran & Co., Inc., 1935.

The Crystal World. London: William Heinemann Ltd., 1937.

The Complete Poems of Richard Aldington. London: Allan Wingate, 1948.

(A selection of poems was also published in German under the title *Bilder* [Hamburg: Angelus Keune, 1947].)

NOVELS, STORIES, AND PLAYS

Death of a Hero. A Novel. New York: Covici, Friede, Inc., 1929.

———. London: Chatto and Windus, 1929.

(Also published in German, Swedish, Danish, French, Russian, Czech, Rumanian, and Spanish. An unexpurgated English edition was published in Paris by Babou & Kahane [1930] and is shortly to be published in England by Consul Books. An English-language edition has also been published in Russia.)

Roads to Glory. London: Chatto and Windus, 1930.

———. Garden City, N.Y.: Doubleday, Doran & Co., Inc., 1930.

Two Stories. London: Elkin Mathews and Marrot, 1930.

At All Costs. London: William Heinemann Ltd., 1930.

Lest Straws. Paris: The Hours Press, 1930.

The Colonel's Daughter. A Novel. London: Chatto and Windus, 1931.

———. Garden City, N.Y.: Doubleday, Doran & Co., Inc., 1931.

(Also published in Danish, Swedish, French, Spanish, Italian, Polish, and Russian.)

Stepping Heavenward. A Record. Florence: G. Orioli, 1931.

———. London: Chatto and Windus, 1931.

Soft Answers. London: Chatto and Windus, 1932.

———. Garden City, N.Y.: Doubleday, Doran & Co., Inc., 1932.

All Men are Enemies. A Romance. London: Chatto and Windus, 1933.

———. Garden City, N.Y.: Doubleday, Doran & Co., Inc., 1933.

(Also published in Danish, Hungarian, Italian, Spanish, Russian, Czech, and Norwegian.)

Women Must Work. A Novel. London: Chatto and Windus, 1934.

———. Garden City, N.Y.: Doubleday, Doran & Co., Inc., 1934.

(Also published in Spanish, Swedish, Italian, Polish, and Czech.)

Life of a Lady. A Play by Richard Aldington and Derek Pat-more. Garden City, N.Y.: Doubleday, Doran & Co., Inc., 1936.

———. London: G. P. Putnam's Sons, 1936.

Very Heaven. London: William Heinemann Ltd., 1937.

———. Garden City, N.Y.: Doubleday, Doran & Co., Inc., 1937.

(Also published in Czech, Italian, and German.)

Seven Against Reeves. A Comedy-Farce. London: William Heinemann Ltd., 1938.

———. Garden City, N.Y.: Doubleday, Doran & Co., Inc., 1938.

(Also published in French, Spanish, and Swedish.)

Rejected Guest. A Novel. New York: The Viking Press, 1939.

———. London: William Heinemann Ltd., [1940?].

The Romance of Casanova. A Novel. New York: Duell, Sloan, and Pearce, 1946.

———. London: William Heinemann Ltd., 1947.

(Also published in Czech, French, Swedish, Spanish, German, and Finnish.)

(A selection of Aldington's short stories was recently published in Russian under the title *Farewell to Memories*.)

ESSAYS, CRITICISM, BIOGRAPHY, AND AUTOBIOGRAPHY

Literary Studies and Reviews. London: George Allen and Unwin Ltd., 1924.

Voltaire. London: George Routledge and Sons Ltd., 1925.

———. New York: E. P. Dutton & Co., 1925.

French Studies and Reviews. London: George Allen and Unwin Ltd., 1926.

———. New York: The Dial Press, 1926.

D. H. Lawrence. An Indiscretion. Seattle: University of Washington Book Store, 1927.

[University of Washington Chapbooks, No. 6.]

D. H. Lawrence. London: Chatto and Windus, 1930.

Remy de Gourmont. A Modern Man of Letters.

————. Seattle: University of Washington Book Store, 1928.

[University of Washington Chapbooks, No. 13.]

Balls and Another Book for Suppression. London: E. Lahr, 1930.

[Blue Moon Booklet, No. 7.]

Balls. Privately printed, 1932.

The Squire. London: William Heinemann Ltd., 1934.

D. H. Lawrence. A Complete List of His Works, Together with a Critical Appreciation. London: William Heinemann Ltd., n.d. [1935?].

Artifex. Sketches and Ideas. London: Chatto and Windus, 1935.

————. Garden City, N.Y.: Doubleday, Doran & Co., Inc., 1936.

W. Somerset Maugham. An Appreciation by Richard Aldington. [with *Sixty-Five*, by W. Somerset Maugham, a Bibliography, an Index of Short Stories, and Appreciations] Garden City, N.Y.: Doubleday, Doran & Co., Inc., 1939.

Life for Life's Sake. A Book of Reminiscences. New York: The Viking Press, 1941.

The Duke, Being an Account of the Life & Achievements of Arthur Wellesley, 1st Duke of Wellington . . . New York: The Viking Press, 1943.

Wellington, Being an Account of the Life & Achievements of Arthur Wellesley, 1st Duke of Wellington . . . London: William Heinemann Ltd., 1946.

(Also published in French, German, Spanish, and Italian.)

Jane Austen. Pasadena: Ampersand Press, 1948.

Four English Portraits, 1801–1851. London: Evans Brothers Ltd., 1948.

The Strange Life of Charles Waterton, 1782–1865. London: Evans Brothers Ltd., 1949.

———. New York: Duell, Sloan, and Pearce, Inc., 1949.

D. H. Lawrence: An Appreciation. Harmondsworth, Middlesex: Penguin Books, 1950.

D. H. Lawrence: Portrait of a Genius But . . . New York: Duell, Sloan, and Pearce, Inc., 1950.

Portrait of a Genius But . . . London: William Heinemann Ltd., 1950.

(Also published in Japanese.)

Pinorman. Personal Recollections of Norman Douglas, Pino Orioli, and Charles Prentice. London: William Heinemann Ltd., 1954.

Ezra Pound and T. S. Eliot. A Lecture. Hurst, Berkshire: Peacocks Press, 1954.

A. E. Housman and W. B. Yeats. Two Lectures. Hurst, Berkshire: Peacocks Press, 1955.

Lawrence L'Imposteur: T. E. Lawrence, The Legend and the Man. Paris: Amiot-Dumont, 1954.

Lawrence of Arabia. A Biographical Inquiry. London: Collins, 1955.

———. Chicago: Henry Regnery, 1955.

Introduction to Mistral. London: William Heinemann Ltd., 1956.

———. Carbondale: Southern Illinois University Press, 1960.

Frauds. London: William Heinemann Ltd., 1957.

A Tourists' Rome. Draguignan, France: Mélissa Press, 1957.

Portrait of a Rebel. The Life and Work of Robert Louis Stevenson.

———. London: Evans Brothers Ltd., 1957.

A Letter from Richard Aldington and a Summary Bibliography of Count Potocki's Published Works. Draguignan, France: Mélissa Press, 1962.

D. H. Lawrence in Selbstzeugnissen und Bilddokumenten. Reinbek bei Hamburg: Rowohlt Taschenbuch Verlag GmbH, 1961.

The Poems of Anyte of Tegea. London: The Egoist Press, 1915.
———. Cleveland: The Clerk's Press, 1917.
[Poets' Translation Series, No. 1.]

Latin Poems of the Renaissance. London: The Egoist Press, 1915.
[Poets' Translation Series, No. 4.]

The Little Demon, by Feodor Sogolub (pseud. of Feodor Teterni-
kov). [Translated by Richard Aldington and John
Cournos.] New York: Alfred A. Knopf, 1916.

The Garland of Months, by Folgore Da San Gemignano. Cleveland: The Clerk's Press, 1917.
[Poets' Translation Series, No. 5.]

Greek Songs in the Manner of Anacreon. London: The Egoist
Press, 1919.
[Poets' Translation Series, Second Set, No. 1.]

The Poems of Meleager of Gadara. London: The Egoist Press,
1920.
[Poets' Translation Series, Second Set, No. 6.]

Medallions in Clay. New York: Alfred A. Knopf, 1921.
Medallions. London: Chatto & Windus, 1931.

*The Good-Humoured Ladies. A Comedy by Carlo Goldoni. . . .
To Which Is Prefix'd an Essay on Carlo Goldoni by
Arthur Symons*. Westminster: C. W. Beaumont, 1922.

French Comedies of the XVIIIth Century. Regnard: *The Residu-
ary Legatee;* Lesage: *Turcaret, or the Financier;* Marivaux:
The Game of Love and Chance; Destouches: *The Con-
ceited Count.*
———. London: George Routledge and Sons Ltd., n.d. [1923].
———. New York: E. P. Dutton and Co., n.d. [1923].
[Broadway Translations.]

Voyages to the Moon and the Sun, by Cyrano de Bergerac. London: George Routledge and Sons Ltd., n.d. [1923].

——. New York: E. P. Dutton and Co., n.d. [1923].
[Broadway Translations.]

Dangerous Acquaintances (Les Liaisons Dangereuses), by
Choderlos de Laclos. London: George Routledge and Sons
Ltd., n.d. [1924].

——. New York: E. P. Dutton and Co., n.d. [1924].
[Broadway Translations.]

Sturly, by Pierre Custot. London: Jonathan Cape Ltd., 1924.

——. Boston: Houghton Mifflin & Co., 1924.

*The Mystery of the Nativity, translated from the Liégeois of the
XVth Century*. London: George Allen and Unwin Ltd.,
1924.

*A Book of 'Characters' From Theophrastus; Joseph Hall, Sir
Thomas Overbury, Nicholas Breton, John Earle, Thomas
Fuller, and other English Authors; Jean De La Bruyere,
Vauvenargues, and Other French Authors*. London:
George Routledge and Sons Ltd., n.d. [1924].

——. New York: E. P. Dutton and Co., n.d. [1924].
[Broadway Translations.]

*The Fifteen Joys of Marriage, Ascribed to Antoine De La Sale,
c. 1388–c. 1462*. London: George Routledge and Sons Ltd.,
n.d. [1926].

——. New York: E. P. Dutton and Co., n.d. [1926].
[Broadway Translations.]

Candide and Other Romances, by Voltaire. London: George
Routledge and Sons Ltd., n.d. [1927].

——. New York: E. P. Dutton and Co., n.d. [1927].
[Broadway Translations.]

Letters of Madame De Sevigné to Her Daughter and Her Friends.
London: George Routledge and Sons Ltd., 1927.

Letters of Voltaire and Frederick the Great. London: George
Routledge and Sons Ltd., 1927.

——. New York: Brentano's, 1927.

[Broadway Library of XVIIIth Century French Literature.]

Letters of Voltaire and Madame du Deffand. London: George
 Routledge and Sons Ltd., 1927.
——. New York: Brentano's, 1927.
[Broadway Library of XVIIIth Century French Literature.]
The Great Betrayal (La Trahison des Clercs), by Julien Benda.
 London: George Routledge and Sons Ltd., 1928.
   The Treason of the Intellectuals. New York: William Mor-
 row & Co., 1928.
Fifty Romance Lyric Poems. New York: Crosby Gaige, 1928.
——. London: Chatto and Windus, 1931.
Remy de Gourmont. Selections from All His Works. New York:
 Covici, Friede, Publishers, 1929.
——. London: Chatto and Windus, 1932.
Alcestis, by Euripides. London: Chatto and Windus, 1930.
The Decameron of Giovanni Boccaccio. New York: Covici,
 Friede, Publishers, 1930.
——. London: G. P. Putnam's Sons, 1930.
Letters to the Amazon, by Remy de Gourmont. London: Chatto
 and Windus, 1931.
Aurelia, by Gérard de Nerval. London: Chatto and Windus,
 1932.
A Wreath for San Gemignano. New York: Duell, Sloan, and
 Pearce, Inc., 1945.
——. London: William Heinemann Ltd., 1946.
Great French Romances: The Princess of Cleves, by Madame de
 Lafayette; *Manon Lescaut,* by the Abbé Prévost; *Danger-
 ous Acquaintances,* by Choderlos de Laclos; *The Duchesse
 de Langeais,* by Honoré de Balzac. London: Pilot Press,
 1946.
——. New York: Duell, Sloan, and Pearce, Inc., 1946.
Larousse Encyclopedia of Mythology. New York: Prometheus
 Press, 1959.
   [Translated by Richard Aldington and Delano Ames; ed.
 Felix Guirard, intro. Robert Graves.]

The Private Life of the Marshal Duke of Richelieu, translated
    by F. S. Flint. London: George Routledge and Sons Ltd.,
    1927.
    [Broadway Library of XVIIIth Century French Literature.]

Memoirs of the Duc de Lauzun, translated, with an appendix,
    by C. K. Scott Moncrieff. London: George Routledge and
    Sons Ltd., 1928.
    [Broadway Library of XVIIIth Century French Literature.]

The Last Voyage, by James Hanley. London: W. Jackson, 1931.
    [Furnival Books, No. 5.]

Apocalypse, by D. H. Lawrence. London: Martin Secker, 1932.

Last Poems, by D. H. Lawrence, edited by Richard Aldington
    and Giuseppe Orioli.

————. Florence: G. Orioli, 1932.

————. New York: The Viking Press, 1933.

————. London: Martin Secker, 1933.

The German Prisoner, by James Hanley. London: Privately
    printed (1933?).

D. H. Lawrence: Selected Poems. London: Martin Secker, 1934.

*The Spirit of Place. An Anthology Compiled from the Prose of
    D. H. Lawrence.* London: William Heinemann Ltd., 1935.

The Viking Book of Poetry of the English-Speaking World.
    New York: The Viking Press, 1941.

    Poetry of the English-Speaking World. London: William
    Heinemann Ltd., 1947.

The Portable Oscar Wilde. New York: The Viking Press, 1946.

    Oscar Wilde. Selected Works. London: William Heinemann
    Ltd., 1946.

Walter Pater. Selected Works. London: William Heinemann
    Ltd., 1948.

———. New York: Duell, Sloan, and Pearce, Inc., 1948.

Pride and Prejudice, by Jane Austen. London: Allan Wingate, 1948.

The Religion of Beauty. Selections from the Aesthetes. London: William Heinemann Ltd., 1950.

A Bibliography of the Works of Richard Aldington from 1915 to 1948, by Alister Kershaw. London: The Quadrant Press, 1950.

———. Burlingame, Calif.: Wm. P. Wreden, 1950.

Mornings in Mexico, by D. H. Lawrence. London: William Heinemann Ltd., 1950.

The White Peacock, by D. H. Lawrence. London: William Heinemann Ltd., 1950.

Selected Letters of D. H. Lawrence. Harmondsworth, Middlesex: Penguin Books, 1950.

[Compiled by Richard Aldington; intro. by Aldous Huxley.]

Aaron's Rod, by D. H. Lawrence. Harmondsworth, Middlesex: Penguin Books, 1950.

Etruscan Places, by D. H. Lawrence. Harmondsworth, Middlesex: Penguin Books, 1950.

Kangaroo, by D. H. Lawrence. Harmondsworth, Middlesex: Penguin Books, 1950.

The Lost Girl, by D. H. Lawrence. Harmondsworth, Middlesex: Penguin Books, 1950.

The Plumed Serpent, by D. H. Lawrence. Harmondsworth, Middlesex: Penguin Books, 1950.

Selected Essays, by D. H. Lawrence. Harmondsworth, Middlesex: Penguin Books, 1950.

St. Mawr, and the Virgin and the Gypsy, by D. H. Lawrence. Harmondsworth, Middlesex: Penguin Books, 1950.

The Woman Who Rode Away, and Other Stories, by D. H. Lawrence. Harmondsworth, Middlesex: Penguin Books, 1950.

The Rainbow, by D. H. Lawrence. Harmondsworth, Middlesex: Penguin Books [1953?].

Sea and Sardinia, by D. H. Lawrence. Harmondsworth, Middlesex: Penguin Books [1953?].

Women in Love, by D. H. Lawrence. Harmondsworth, Middlesex: Penguin Books [1953?].

Italy. A Book of Photographs. London: Anglo-Italian Publication [1958?].

Austria. A Book of Photographs. London: Anglo-Italian Publication [1958?].

France. A Book of Photographs. London: Anglo-Italian Publication [1958?].

Switzerland. A Book of Photographs. London: Spring Books [1958?].

D. H. Lawrence: A Composite Biography, Vol. III, ed. Edward Nehls. Madison: University of Wisconsin Press, 1959.

Rome: A Book of Photographs. London: Spring Books, 1960.

D. H. Lawrence: l'œuvre et la vie, by F.-J. Temple. Paris: Seghers, 1960.